CHILDREN'S COSTUME IN ENGLAND

Children in the fashion of the 1840s

Detail from A Group of Children *by John Phillip*, R.A.

CHILDREN'S COSTUME IN ENGLAND

From the Fourteenth to the end of the Nineteenth Century

PHILLIS CUNNINGTON
& ANNE BUCK

LONDON
ADAM & CHARLES BLACK

FIRST PUBLISHED 1965

BY A. AND C. BLACK LIMITED

4, 5 AND 6 SOHO SQUARE LONDON W.1

© 1965 PHILLIS CUNNINGTON & ANNE BUCK

Printed in Great Britain by
W. & J. Mackay & Co Ltd, Chatham, Kent

CONTENTS

THE PLATES

Acknowledgements

We should like to thank the following individuals and institutions for their help: Miss J. Arnold, Mr. D. K. Baxandall, Lady Cox, Miss E. Cunnington, Mr. F. G. Emmision, Miss J. Godber, Miss Z. Halls, Mr. R. E. Hutchison, Miss P. Leach, Mrs. S. Luckham, Major A. Mansfield, Mr. S. Maxwell, Mr. J. L. Nevinson; The British Museum Library, Print and Manuscript Rooms, The National Portrait Gallery, The National Buildings Record, The Witt and Conway Libraries of the Courtauld Institute of Art and the many museums who have made their collections available for study. We owe a special debt of gratitude to Dr. E. J. Dingwall and Miss C. Lucas.

THE FOURTEENTH CENTURY

Contemporary evidence, written or pictorial, of children's clothing in this century is extremely rare and little girls appear to be almost entirely ignored. What we do know, however, is that the baby, male or female, started life by being swaddled.

> "When the child is born
> He must be swaddled."
>   Early fourteenth century. (*The Treatise of Walter de Biblesworth*.)

Swaddling involved bandaging the baby's body from neck to toe, enclosing the arms and legs in a solid bundle, apparently owing to a fear that the limbs might get damaged or even fall off by careless handling unless thus protected. And:

> "To protect his clothes from slobber
> You will say to his nurse
> 'Make the child a bib'." (Ibid.)

Family group. Swaddled baby carried by mother, small child on another woman's back, boy in loose tunic following the father. 1320. (*Queen Mary's Psalter*.)

As regards little boys, Walter de Biblesworth tells them:

"Put on your clothes dear children
Draw on your braies, shoes, gloves,
Put on your hood, cover your head,
Button your buttons and then again
Gird yourself with a leather belt."

Braies were loose-fitting drawers tied round the waist with a running string. They were in the nature of an undergarment but were visible if worn with a short tunic or with a long, when hitched up for convenience, for example when climbing trees.

The tunic was the child's frock. It was usually ankle length, but might reach only to mid-calf and was sometimes slit up in front for a short distance from the hem. The sleeves were often loose, ending well above the wrist. *Super-tunico* were similar.

The *leather belt* or girdle was not always worn by boys but was a usual adjunct and was fastened by a buckle.

"The tip of the girdle's end passes through the buckle."

(*W. de Biblesworth.*)

(*a*) Boy in brown super-tunic with red stripes, red coif under blue hood, red tunic and red socks.

(*b*) Dancing boy with blue hood and red lining, blue lining to super-tunic, grey stockings, *c.* 1330. (*Both from Holkham Bible Picture Book.*)

The hood was an essential part of the child's wardrobe. It had a loose pointed cowl with attached cape reaching to the shoulders. *The Cape*, known as the *gorget*, was closed all round so that the hood had to be put on over the head; but it was frequently thrown back, the hood portion dangling behind, whilst anchored by the gorget which swathed the neck. In the fourteenth century the pointed cowl of the hood was prolonged into a hanging tail known as a liripipe. With children this was generally rather short. The hood was often lined with a bright colour visible round the face portion.

Shoes were shaped to the foot, distinguishing right from left. They fitted round the ankle, covering the foot, and were laced on the inner side similarly to those of their parents.

Gloves were worn by all classes and children's gloves were probably made on the same pattern as those of adults. The gloves were made of leather or of a thick coarse material and finished with a spreading gauntlet cuff.

Small boy in tunic and wearing a hood with short liripipe. Fourteenth century. (From a mediaeval tile in the British Museum.)

In the second half of the fourteenth century new styles evolved and boys of the upper classes, having grown out of infancy, were dressed like their fathers.

The gipon, called a doublet in the next century, now replaced the tunic and was worn next the shirt. The gipon was padded and slightly shaped in to the waist, falling without gathers to mid-thigh or a little lower. It was either buttoned or laced down the front. The neck was low and round and the sleeves were tight, with buttons from elbow to wrist. When worn without an overgarment the gipon was belted at hip level; waist level was unfashionable. Noblemen and their sons wore the "knightly girdle" (1350–1410) which was a belt made up of decorative metal plaques, fastened in front by an ornamental buckle.

> "John was liberally fitted out with furs. . . . When he was eight years old he was given a silver gilt belt fashioned in the shape of harebells and two years later he had a sword."
> 1397. (*My Lord of Bedford, 1389–1435* by Carlton Williams, 1963, quoting from Duchy of Lancaster Wardrobe Accts 28/0/6 and 28/4/1/.)

Boy aged 8 years in gipon, knightly girdle, sleeves buttoned from elbow to knuckles, dagged mantle, long hose. Ankle shoes with inner lacing 1344. (Effigy of William of Hatfield, York Minster.)

Leg wear now consisted of tight-fitting thigh-length *hose* which were tied to the under side of the gipon. The gipon was provided with pairs of strings to thread through corresponding eyelet holes in the hose. The ties were called *points* and this method of attaching the hose to the gipon and later to the doublet was known as "trussing the points". The close fit of the hose was obtained by material cut on the cross. Hose were sometimes soled and could then be worn without shoes.

Boy's *shoes* were now open over the instep with ankle straps. Noblemen's sons might have shoes with punched-out designs as a form of decoration.

Two youths in sleeveless supertunics called tabards. Tunic sleeves emerging. Two young girls in long kirtles with girdles. 1320. (*Queen Mary's Psalter*.)

Shoes began to be slightly pointed about 1360 but the piked shoes did not come into fashion until *c.* 1395.

Outdoor garments were ankle-length *cloaks* or thigh-length *capes*. These when worn by noblemen's sons were often decorated by *dagging*, or *jagging*, that is having their edges cut into elaborate scallops. On the head, hoods were still worn and on ceremonial occasions a boy might wear a *chaplet* which was a jewelled metal circlet, worn by both sexes.

Hair was arranged with or without a centre parting and fell down to neck level.

C.C.E.–B

Little girls in the fourteenth century are rarely depicted or described. From the few examples found we know that they were dressed in long plain gowns or *kirtles*, as they were called, slightly moulding the figure like those worn by their mothers and reaching the ground. But children's neck line was less décolletée and sleeves were moderately loose. The kirtle was fastened behind by lacing from neck to waist level.

Young girl in long kirtle embroidered at hem, veil on head. Fourteenth century. (*Book of Hours*, Egerton MS, British Museum.) From the Presentation of the Virgin Mary in the Temple.

Over the kirtle might be worn a *cote-hardie*, an overgarment common to both sexes. It was close-fitting and long to the ankles. The neck was low, the garment being put on over the head without fastenings, although some were made to button down the front. The distinguishing feature of the cote-hardie was the construction of the sleeves. These were elbow-length and then continued on behind into tongue-shaped hanging flaps which, by the second half of the century, were extended into long narrow streamers called *tippets*. Vertical placket holes in the skirt called *fitchets* were common, but no girdle was worn.

In the trousseau of Princess Joan aged 14, is mentioned:

"a double (i.e. lined) coate-hardie for riding". 1347.

Another garment worn over the kirtle was the *sideless surcoat* lasting until about 1500. It was low-necked and sleeveless with wide gaps under the arms down to hip level. Isabella of Valois was only 9 when she married Richard II in 1377 and her trousseau included a sideless surcoat of red velvet embossed with birds of goldsmith's work, perched on branches woven in pearls and emeralds; the

Salome shown as a young girl in a sideless surcoat. Fourteenth century.
(*Holkham Bible Picture Book*.)

border of the gown was miniver. (*What They Wore*, a History of Children's Dress by Margaret Jackson (Allen & Unwin).)

Little girls' *headwear* was either a *coif* or a *veil* though, unlike their mothers, children frequently went bare-headed. The coif, common to both sexes, was a plain close-fitting linen bonnet curving round to cover the ears and tied under the chin. The veil was a white scarf, draped over the head and falling behind on to the shoulders.

Out of doors hooded cloaks were worn. Shoes resembled those worn by their brothers.

Hair styles for girls were very similar to those of their brothers, but from a centre parting the hair might be arranged in roll curls above the ears.

How far older daughters copied their mothers' "make up" we do not know. Eyebrow plucking and face painting were fashionable from *c.* 1370 to 1480 and we do know that the French Knight of the Tour Landry advised his daughters against this.

> "Fair daughters, see that you pluck not away the hairs from your eyebrows, nor from your temples, nor from your foreheads, to make them appear higher than Nature ordained." (1371–2.)

Young girl aged 13 years wearing a long sideless surcoat and veil, *c.* 1310. (From a wall painting at Croughton Church, Northants, representing the Virgin Mary leaving home to be betrothed.)

THE FIFTEENTH CENTURY

THE FIFTEENTH CENTURY

The swaddling of babies continued as described in the previous chapter and remained the custom well into the eighteenth century.

Christening robes for infants of the aristocracy and royalty were extremely grand:

> "The child must be wrapped in a velvet cloak . . . which must be at least three ells long, and must be furred with miniver, and when the child is wrapped in the velvet, then must be put over the child (when the person carrying it has it on her arm) a long couvrechef or kerchief of violet silk extending from the child's head down to the ground, and at the feet end as long as the cloak or longer."
> (Quoted in *What They Wore* by Margaret Jackson (Allen & Unwin).)

.   .   .

Small boys wore loose *gowns* hanging straight down to the ankles. No belt was worn by children. Thus they differed from their fathers who considered it a sign of degradation to be deprived of a belt or

Little Isaac in long gown, close sleeves.
Fifteenth century. (Ex Dyson Perrins M.S.
Illustrations of the Bible.)

more rarely, a sign of humility until *c.* 1450. The child's gown fitted round the neck and was either fastened by buttons a short way down the front, or less often by buttons over the left shoulder. The sleeves were long, being rather loose and of equal width from shoulder to wrist.

Gowns for older boys might be long or short to the knees and in the second half of the century a low stand-collar with rounded corners sloping to a V under the chin, was sometimes worn.

> "A shorte gowne made of 2 yerds and 3 quarters of crymysyn clothe of gold, lined with 2 yerds 3 quarters of blac velvet; a longe gowne made of 6 yerds of grene damaske; a shorte gowne made of 2 yerds 3 quarters of purpull velvet, lyned with 2 yerds di' grene damask. . . . A ryding gowne lyned with 2 yerds and 3 quarters of blac satyn. . . ."
>
> 1483. (*Grose Antiquarian Repository*, Vol. I.)

This was part of the wardrobe assigned to Lord Edward aged 13 "Son of the late Kyng Edward the Fourthe". Less costly gowns

Boy aged 12 years, in long gown with round neck close sleeves, and front vent to skirt. Ankle shoes buckled. 1470. (Tomb of John Stanley, Church of St. Peter, Elford, Staffs.)

might be made of wool or "frieze", "that ze wille do byen sume frese to maken of zour child is gowns". 1449. (*The Paston Letters.*)

.   .   .

Older boys wore the man's suit of the period consisting of a doublet and hose. The doublet was the term used from *c.* 1400 to 1670 re-placing but corresponding to the gipon. A short gown might be worn over this suit.

The doublet now, was close-fitting, well padded, waisted and short, the doublet skirt barely reaching the upper thighs. The sleeves were close-fitting and the neck had a stand-collar from *c.* 1450 to 1490 when a low square neck line was introduced. It was belted at hip level when worn alone, as in the fourteenth century, but by the second half of the fifteenth century waist level was the rule. It was laced down the front from 1400 to 1450 or fastened by buttons or hooks and eyes after 1425.

After 1450 some doublets were made with a deep V opening in front discarding the stand-collar and the gap was filled by a panel called a *stomacher*, over which the doublet was laced up. This style was worn by the young Lord Edward:

"A doublet and a stomacher made of 2 yerds of blac satyn." 1483.

Schoolboys in long beltless houppelandes. One wears a doublet, long hose and piked shoes. 1481. (Caxton's *Mirrour of the World*, British Museum.)

Other materials for doublets were damask, velvet, or for ordinary wear, broadcloth, fustian, linen, and sometimes leather. A mixture of materials was sometimes used when the doublet was hidden by the gown. Then the visible portions such as the sleeves and collars of the doublet might be of richer material than that of the body. The method of fastening the doublet to the hose by "trussing the points" continued as in the fourteenth century.

The Gown called a *Houppelande*, was a garment worn over the doublet and hose. With adults it was generally ankle or ground-length and then usually ceremonial; but with boys it was often short to the knees or above and probably worn for warmth. The neck unlike that of adults, was round and close-fitting with a low stand-collar, but later the collar was discarded. It was fastened down the front from neck to hem by buttons or hooks and eyes, these being concealed under the folds of the gown. The sleeves were plain cylindrical of equal width from shoulder to wrist or what were known as bagpipe or pokys sleeves. These hung down from a closed wrist forming a huge hanging pouch which was sometimes used as a pocket. Hanging sleeves so common with adults, appeared for

David wearing a short, belted, houppelande with bag-pipe sleeves. 1414–22. (*Duke of Bedford's Psalter and Book of Hours,* British Museum.)

children in the sixteenth century. A belt at waist level or just below was always worn.

Materials for houppelandes were wool, velvet, satin or damask and fur trimmings were common. These gowns were always lined.

Leg wear of the fifteenth century consisted of long stockings called hose, which spread up the thighs, were joined at the fork and prolonged over the hips at first barely covering the seat but reaching the waist by the end of the century. Materials and colours varied. Young Lord Edward was provided with:

> "2 pair of hosen made of a yerde and a quarter of broode meighlyn★ blac." 1483.

> William Paston junior writing from Etonto his brother John said: "Also I beseche you to sende me a hose clothe, one for the halydays of sum colore, and anothyr for the workyng days, how corse so ever it be it makyth no matyr; and a stomechere and 2 schyrtes, and a peyer of sclyppers" (slippers). 1478.

The Codpiece (1408–1575) was a small pouch with a front flap at the fork, fastened by ties.

Separate *hose* like long stockings were now rarely worn except by

Boy in short-skirted doublet, sleeves puffed out above. He wears long hose.

★ Fustian from Milan.

labourers and their sons, who sometimes wore short hose gartered below the knee. These would only be worn with short belted gowns. Soled hose continued to be worn without shoes and *pattens* were added in wet weather. These were also listed among other accessories in Lord Edward's wardrobe.

> "7 pair of shoon of Spaingnysh leder (Spanish leather) double soled . . . and a pair of patyns." 1483.

Fifteenth-century *pattens* were also worn with shoes and were the height of fashion from 1440 to 1460 when they were worn regardless of the weather, indoors as well as out. They had wooden soles, usually made of aspen because of its lightness, with raised cross-bars at heel and toe. They were shaped to the prevailing fashion of shoe but longer. Black leather straps were added to buckle over the instep or they were secured by a "saddle" over the foot.

Children's shoes followed the design of their elders but the piked shoes fashionable between 1395 and 1410 and again between 1460 and 1480 were worn only by older boys. All through the fifteenth century shoes were in the nature of low boots, clasping the ankle and closed by strap and buckle or sometimes by lacing at the sides or centre. Ankle-strapped shoes of the fourteenth century continued also for a few years. *Slippers* are also mentioned in Lord Edward's inventory but exactly what they were is not known. They were probably a light form of low shoe easily slipped on and off and worn indoors.

> "2 pair of slippers of blac leder,
> 2 pair of slippers of Spaignysh leder." 1483.

The price of children's shoes is shown as follows, in the shoe-maker's bill to Sir William Stonor:

> "It. to my lady's chyldryn 18 peyre
>   price of all the peyrs 3s.
> It. to the chylde of the botery 8 peyre,
>   price the peyre 4d."
>
> 1478–9. (*The Stonor Letters*, Vol. 2.)

Head wear for boys consisted of caps, bonnets, hats and hoods. The cap resembled a coif. The bonnet had a small close-fitting crown, with a close-fitting turn-up brim. The hat was larger, with a wider brim and a crown that varied. It might be tall, round or tapering. The hood remained unchanged from the fourteenth century.

> "As for cappys that ye sent me for the chyldren, they be to lytyl for hem. I pray yow bey hem feyner cappys and larger than tho wer."
>
> 1450. (*The Paston Letters.*)

> "When thi betters speke to the
> Do offe thi cape and bow the knee."
>
> c. 1475. (*The Babees Book.*)

Lord Edward was provided with:

> "a bonet made of 3 quarters of a yerde of purpull velvette"

as well as "13 bonets" and "5 hatts". 1483. He also had "5 paire gloves".

But though there was considerable variety in boys' head wear, to go bare-headed was quite usual especially with young boys. *Hair style* was short and curly or waving to the nape of the neck.

Of *accessories*, as in the previous century, children were provided with handkerchiefs, known as "muckinders" or more politely "hand-cloths" or "hand-coverchiefs".

.　　.　　.

Girls as far as is known were dressed like their mothers, with some modifications, but description of their clothing is mostly confined to royalty, when the garments worn would be of a rich ceremonial nature. However the terms used indicate the type of garments worn by all at that time.

Over the chemise or smock, to use the correct term at this date, a girl's dress would consist of the *kirtle*, still sometimes called a *tunic*, over which might be worn a *sideless surcoat* also called a *super tunic*. Alternatively a *gown* or *houppelande* might be worn over the kirtle which was seldom worn alone. Sometimes, if the gown was heavy, detachable kirtle sleeves only would be worn, emerging from the wide sleeves of the gown.

The kirtle or tunic was close-fitting and low-necked with long tight sleeves sometimes extending over the back of the hand. It was laced up in front or behind.

The child wears a sideless surcoat, *c.* 1425. From the Statue of St. Anne and the Virgin in the Crypt of York Minster.

The sideless surcoat or super tunic (1360–1500) was low-necked and sleeveless, being cut away widely under the arms from shoulder to hip, thus exposing to view much of the undergarment. It fell in folds to the ground as did all female garments.

The gown was a more enveloping garment with a flat turn-down collar and wide funnel-shaped sleeves through which the kirtle sleeves emerged.

The trousseaux of Princess Philippa, youngest daughter of Henry Duke of Lancaster and later King Henry IV, has been recorded. She was married by proxy at the age of 12. The following is a list of some of the garments provided.

Wedding Dress: 1406.
"A tunic and mantle with a long train of white satin worked with velvet, furred with pured minever and purfled (edged) with ermine and the sleeves of the tunic also furred with ermine."

Then there were five gowns.

(1) "of cloth of gold of Cyprus worked with white flowers and furred with pured minever".

(2) "red velvet embroidered with pearls, furred with pured minever and purfled with ermine".

(3) "red cloth of gold of Cyprus worked with white roses, furred with pured minever and purfled with ermine".

(4) "a long gown of cloth of gold of Cyprus having a white ground worked with blue flowers".

(5) "of green cloth, lined with green tartarin".

Another set comprised "a blue velvet tunic, an open super-tunic and mantle with a train furred with pured minever and purfled with ermine". There were also four tunics worn with gowns of green cloth, one of scarlet, and one of black cloth.

The mantle was purely a ceremonial garment and only worn by a child on this special occasion. Princess Philippa's was:

"A gown and mantle with a trayil (train) of blue and green cloth of gold of Cyprus worked with egles of gold, and furred with pured minever." She also had "a mantle of blue cloth furred with pured minever" and "a mantle of cloth of gold", also "a pair of sleeves" of cloth of gold. 1406. (Trousseau of Princess Philippa, Archaeologia Vol. 57.)

Where little girls differed from their mothers appears to be in their *head dresses* which, with adults, were varied and complicated throughout this century. Princess Philippa was allotted:

"five silk chaplets . . . a cap of beaver furred with ermine, garnished with a silk button and tassel. A hood of scarlet cloth and a hood of black cloth, both furred with pured minever."

The *chaplet* was a circlet set with gems and worn on festive occasions or a wreath of twisted silk or satin or merely a padded ornamental roll. The cap might have been a *Turkey bonnet*, a tall fez-shaped cap worn by both sexes.

Perhaps the most popular style of gown for young as well as old from about 1470 was one which moulded the figure to the waist or hips then falling in full folds to the ground. Some were made with a seam at the waist which was a new form of construction appearing at this time. The neck line was very low, edged with a falling collar which was narrow and frequently furred to match similarly decorated cuffs when present.

Sleeves were tight-fitting to the wrist. The belt was narrow and worn loosely round the waist and was often finished with a long hanging end. The gown was generally laced down the front.

Hair styles for little girls continued as for the fourteenth century, but older girls of a marriageable age might have flowing locks falling to the waist or lower.

Girl in low-necked gown shaped to the figure and narrow belt. She has her hair flowing loose and wears a Turkey bonnet. 1479. (Brass of the family of Sir T. Urswyck at Dagenham.)

THE SIXTEENTH CENTURY

THE SIXTEENTH CENTURY

As in the previous century, all children started life swathed in swaddling clothes. A shirt was worn under the swaddling bands and from time to time during the day the swaddling was removed and the child was dressed in garments giving some freedom to the limbs. This is shown in a delightful extract from M. St. Clare Byrne's *Elizabethan Home* in which she has unearthed dialogues by Claudius Hollyband and Peter Erondell, two Huguenot refugees who taught French in London in the 1560's. From Dialogue 5, In the Nursery, by Peter Erondell:

> "*The Lady to the Nurse*: How now, how doth the childe? . . . Unswaddle him, undoe his swadling bands, . . . wash him before me. . . . Pull off his shirt, thou art pretty and fat my little darling. . . . Now swadle him againe, But first put on his biggin and his little band (collar) with an edge, where is his little petticote? Give him his coate of changeable (shot) taffata and his sattin sleeves: Where is his bibbe? Let him have his gathered aprone with stringes, and hang a Muckinder (handkerchief) to it. You need not yet to give him his corall with the small golden chayne, for I believe it is better to let him sleepe untill the afternoone. . . ." (1568.)

Swaddled infant—Richard Best, d. 1587. (Merstham Church, Surrey.)

Babies and infants always wore *biggins* which were similar to coifs. A boy's cap, when required, would be worn over this. The boy's cap was usually shaped like a "pork-pie" hat trimmed with a feather, but some had a high crown with a narrow turned-up brim.

In Thomas Deloney, *The Gentle Craft*, 1597–1600, the midwife gives a list of her needs: "sope and candles, beds shirts, biggins,

Baby boy in gown with wings and hanging sleeves, bib under chin, muckinder hanging from waist, wearing a coif under a small cap. *c.* 1563. (Catherine, Countess of Hertford and her infant son, Audley End, Essex—copy of original at Petworth House.)

wastcoats, headbands, swadelbands, crosseclothes, bibs, tailclouts, mantles, hose, shooes, coats, petticoats, cradle and crickets".*

It is interesting to note how often these infants were portrayed holding a stick of *coral*, with or without attached bells, both of which were good luck symbols. The stick of coral was later considered useful for teething purposes. In 1490 Antonio Solaris's painting of the Madonna and Child, with St. John the Baptist, depicts the Infant Christ with a coral cross at the neck!

* Crickets: low stools.

During the second half of the century and possibly earlier, children of the aristocracy, after swaddling was discarded, were robed in long skirted gowns often of heavy ornate and embroidered materials. This gown was sometimes sleeveless, the arm holes having wings only and the remains of hanging sleeves in the form of pendant streamers. *Wings* (c. 1545–1640s) were stiffened bands or rolls, often very decorative, projecting over the shoulder seam and resembling epaulettes. The pendant streamers attached to the back of the arm holes, were used as leading strings when the child was learning to walk. The sleeveless gown might have detachable or shirt sleeves emerging, trimmed with frills called *ruffles*, at the wrist. The

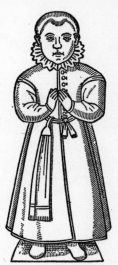

Small boy in long gown, buttoned to waist, with muckinder hanging from girdle. 1585. (Brass of Peter Best, Merstham Church, Surrey.)

neck also had ruffles. The gown with its own sleeves might have ruffles or a turn-down collar called a *falling band,* or simply *band,* at the neck and ruffles or cuffs at the wrist. A bib was worn under the chin and a large muckinder was frequently pinned on at the waist to hang down on one side in front. With children from six months to a year *aprons* with bibs were usually worn.

Little boys up to the age of 6 or 7 were dressed in ankle-length gowns, belted at the waist. In the first half of the century the neck was low revealing the frilled neck of the shirt, and the shirt sleeves emerged through the hanging sleeves of the gown. Wings were almost invariably present. After *c.* 1550, the gown, which was buttoned down to waist level, usually had its own sleeves and the neck and wrist were frilled. After 1560, small *ruffs* and *hand-ruffs* replaced the frills.

Edward Prince of Wales, son of Henry VIII, aged 1–2 years, in gown with hanging sleeves, wearing coif under flat cap. Broad-toed shoes. 1538–9. (Holbein School. Syon House, Duke of Northumberland Collection.)

Boys of 7 or 8 might still be wearing skirts, but the body garment would be a doublet. Even with this costume a sword could be worn.

. . .

After little boys had been "breeched", they were dressed like their fathers, in suits comprising a *doublet*, a *jerkin* (with children sometimes called a coat), a *gown* and *hose*. Cloaks were worn out of doors.

The *doublet* (a term used from about 1400 to 1670) was the main body garment, worn over the shirt, or over the waistcoat which was a quilted under doublet worn in cold weather. The doublet varied in cut according to the fashion of the day, but it was always close-fitting, and waisted. Some doublets had detachable sleeves which were fastened at the armholes by points, i.e. ties which were hidden by an overgarment, or after 1545 by wings. Detachable sleeves were always listed separately in contemporary inventories. Doublet sleeves were always closed at the wrist, but the upper portion varied from being close-fitting throughout or ballooned above the elbow. The length of the doublet skirt also varied from being a very narrow border to a skirt reaching to the thighs. In the early part of the century the skirt might be absent; during the second half it tended to be short. The neck was low until about 1540. Subsequently a stand-collar was added. Doublets were padded and fastened down the front to the waist by buttons, hidden hooks and eyes, lacing, or tied by points. Doublet materials varied and were sometimes

Charles Stewarde, aged 6 years, wearing long gown with winged sleeves and hand ruffs. Small neck ruff. His brother, Lord Darnley, aged 17, in the fashion of the day. 1563. (Copyright reserved to H.M. the Queen.)

different from the rest of the suit though always of a harmonising colour. Velvet, satin, taffeta, or brocade were fashionable but simpler stuff was also used.

> "For Francis (a small boy) Payde to the taylor of Walden for bockeram for a fustyan dublet 6d, for three nayles of fustyan for the same 11d."
>
> 1550. (Report on the MSS. of Lord Middleton. Account of George Medley, Guardian of the children Francis and Margaret.)

> "For two yeardes of lynnen cloth to lyne upper bodyez and dublettes."
>
> 1550. (Ibid.)

From the clothing expenses of Sir William Petre's children and others, Ingatestone Hall, Essex, we find:

> "Item payd to Randall for a doussen di' (half) of buttons for Johan* and Gorge† cotes of fryzaddo (a heavy worsted cloth like baize)

James I of England, VI of Scotland, aged 8 years. Sleeveless jerkin with double wings "in pickadil". Closed ruff and hand ruffs to doublet sleeves. Full Venetians. High bonnet trimmed with feathers. 1574. (National Portrait Gallery, unknown artist.)

---

* John Petre, born 1549.
† George Fermer, a schoolboy lodger.

PLATE I

Elizabeth, wife of Henry VII, and daughters, the last two with hair loose. (Youngest aged *c.* 10). All wear draped hoods, ceremonial mantles fastened with tasselled cords, over gown and kirtle with fur cuffs matching the lining and trimming of the mantles. 1500–1503.

Duke of Northumberland Collection, Syon House
Reproduced by permission of Country Life

PLATE 2

Princess (later Queen) Elizabeth, aged 13. Bodice with low
decolletage. Oversleeves expanding over large undersleeves
which match the forepart of the skirt worn over a Spanish
farthingale. Narrow jewelled girdle. French hood with upper
and nether billiments. *c.* 1545–6.

Reproduced by gracious permission of Her Majesty the Queen

2d. ob' quarter. For a skayne of blacke sylke for holles 2d. Item for a di' ownse of Russet sylke for thyr doublettes 8d."

1556–7. (Essex Record Office, D/DP.A.15. Transcript D/DPZ.14/2.)

The jerkin, sometimes called a *cote* or *jacket*, was worn over the doublet and was lined but not padded. It was shaped like the doublet with a varying length of skirt which, however, was always slightly longer than that of the doublet. Boys' jerkins were usually sleeveless similar to those worn by adults.

"A common garment daylye used such as we call a jerkin or jacket without sleeves."

1599. (*Thynne's Animadversions*.)

But some had sleeves variously puffed out above the elbow thence

Three small boys wearing sleeveless jerkins, with doublet sleeves emerging, and small feather-trimmed bonnets. Instead of ruffs they wear small falling bands. 1568. (Detail Lord Windsor and family by Eworth. Owner the Marquess of Bute, Mount Stuart Rothsay, Isle of Bute.)

straight to the wrist. Attached hanging sleeves were sometimes present. Detachable sleeves were also worn. The jerkin was buttoned, laced or tied down the front. The materials varied, such as taffeta and damask, but leather was popular.

"For makying of his★ taffyta coate (i.e. jerkin) 5d."

1550. (Lord Middleton MS.)

"For an ell of fustyan to make Francis slevez 12d. . . . for makyng a damaske coate and a payre of sleeves 12d."

(Ibid.)

"For a skynne and a halfe to make Mr. Frances a jerkyn 3s. Item for russating of the same 6d. Item for making of the same 8d."

1552. (Ibid.)

"Item for a Spanyssh skynne for a jerkyn for Mr. Frances. . . ."

1552. (Ibid.)

"For a Rone skyne to make my brother Frances a jerkyn 2s. 4d."

1553. (Ibid.)

"For a doussen di' of buttons for Johan and Gorge coates of fryzaddo 2d. ob' quarter."

1556. (Petre Accounts, Essex Record Office, D/D.P.A. 15.)

"For buttons bowght for the boyes cotes 10d."

1556. (Petre Accounts.)

Boy, aged 5 years, in long gown with stand collar edged with pickadils, i.e. ornamental tabs, sometimes used to support a ruff. 1584. (Tomb of Robert Dudley, infant son of the Earl of Leicester. "The Noble Imp", St. Mary's Church, Warwick.)

★ The boy Francis.

At the neck ruffs, which were the fashion from 1550s to 1640s, were worn by children from about the age of 5 years. These had to be supported by a fairly high stand-collar and in some cases by the addition of a tabbed border, the tabs being called "pickadils".

> "For halfe an ell of cloth for ruffez for my brother Frances and me 13d."
>
> 1553. (Written by Margaret Willoughby. Middleton Accounts.)

Francis Bacon, aged 12 years. Jerkin with short puffed sleeves edged with pickadils as is the neck. Small ruff open in front and attached to shirt. *c.* 1573. (From life-size painted terra cotta bust of Francis Bacon at Gorhambury, The Earl of Verulam.)

The *gown* at this period was not the main frock as worn by infants but an overgarment of a somewhat dressy nature. It was worn over the doublet or jerkin, was broad-shouldered and fell in ample folds to just above or just below the knees. With adults it was longer. It was open all down the front and the borders were often edged with fur or trimmed with embroidery.

> "Item payd to the scynner for furrynge of 2 gownes of sacke clothe after 20d. the pece for Johan* (aged 7) and Gorget† 3s. 4d.
> Item to the same gownes for a xii, whyte hares at 16d. a pece 14s. 8d.
> Item to the same gowns xviii whyte lambe skynes at 3d. the pece 4s. 6d."
>
> 1556. (Petre Accounts.)

* John, born 1549, son of Sir Wm. Petre.
† A schoolboy lodger.

Materials varied:

> "For 3 quarters of brode cloth for a gowne for Frances 6s. 8d. For a
> yeard and a halfe of black cotton for a gown 12d."
>
> 1550. (Middleton Accounts.)

> "For a pece of blacke buckeram contaynynge 15 yerdes for the
> chyldren gownes 10s.8d."
>
> 1556. (Petre Accounts.)

Some had a flat square collar falling behind called a cape. The sleeves
were usually hanging sleeves, long and tubular with an opening in
the upper part for the arm to emerge. Some had a puffed-out
shoulder sleeve with an attached ornamental hanging sleeve.

Prince, later King Edward VI, aged
about 8 years, wearing doublet and
sleeves with slashed design. Fur edged
short gown with hanging sleeves. Upper
stocks with slashed pattern. Flat cap and
feather. *c.* 1545. (Audley End, Essex.
Copy of original Holbein at Windsor
Castle—and made full length.) A long
list of Prince Edward's garments as a
child is contained in Warrants
Wardrobe Accounts, 35th Henry
VIII, 1543. P.R.O.E. 101.423/11/2.

"For makyng a gowne 11s, for a quarter of russell (a Norwich fabric of worsted with a lustrous satin-like finish) for the same 5d. for fustyan for the bodyez 8d. for halfe a yearde of cotton for the plytez (pleats); for claspez 1d."

1550. (Middleton MS.)

Black gowns and hoods were worn by children as well as by adults at funerals.

"To make them gownes and hodes after the maner and facon (fashion) of morners . . . I wille that everyone of my children have gownes and hodes of blake clothe."

1529. (Will of Sir David Owen. Sussex Arch. Colln., Vol. VII.)

The *night gown* was a long loose gown worn for warmth and comfort with the hose, but not worn over the doublet. It was not, as the name suggests, a garment worn at night. It was often of rich material. It would only be worn by older boys. The following is an account for a Scottish boy's night gown and hose.

"Boy—*nightgowne and hois*
5 elns lylis wirset . . . to be ane nicht gowne to my lord governour's sone David £3. 10. 0.
½ eln welwett to wait the samyn 35/-
buckeram to wait the samyn 2/-
To . . . for furring the samyn £2. 10. 0.
3 quarters gray stemmyng of myllane (a fine worsted from) Milan) to be hym hois £1. 10. 0.
for cloth to lyne the samyn hois with 5/-
One dosane of Poyntis 2/-
for making of this gowne and hois 10/-
5 quarters of canvas to turn them to 10/-"

1551. (Accounts of the Lord High Treasurer of Scotland.

Leg wear was of two kinds: (1) Hose, worn throughout the century and (2) Knee breeches.

The term hose in this period always meant leg wear and not stockings, except for girls. (It began to indicate stockings about 1660.) The boy's hose, up till about 1540, consisted of long tights as in the fifteenth century, the upper portion round the buttocks being known as the upper stocks or breech, the lower portion being called the nether stocks. The term "upper stocks" went out of use in the 1550s when the breech was ovally distended to mid-thigh, by padding called bombast and generally decorated by panes. These were long vertical slits through which a contrasting white or coloured lining might be seen, a favourite form of decoration from 1500 to 1650s. After 1550 the breech was enormously distended or rather "bombasted", the bombast consisting of any or all of the following: wool, rags, flax, flocks, horsehair, cotton or even bran.

"For a quarterne of bumbaste 3d."

1556. (Petre Accounts.)

This style of leg wear was then called *trunk hose, trunk breeches, round hose, French hose* or *trunk slops*. The term slops is confusing as it has been applied to a number of different garments. Palsgrave, who died in 1554, wrote "Sloppe—a nightgown." But a pair of slops or trunk slops always indicates bombasted trunk hose.

"For a payre of sloppez for my nepveu Fraunces 6d. . . . for lynyng the same 9d."

1550. (Middleton Accounts.)

After 1570 a new style was introduced in which the nether stocks

Small boy in sleeveless jerkin with wings. High collar and ruff. Hand ruffs to doublet sleeves. Bombasted trunk hose. Shoes decorated with "pinking". Tall bonnet trimmed with feather. *c.* 1575. (Chatsworth Devonshire Collections. Portrait at Hardwick wrongly labelled James V of Scotland.)

ceased to cover the feet but ended as thigh fitting extensions from the trunk hose, to the knees or just below. These extensions were called *canions* and separate stockings had to be drawn up over them. Whether boys ever wore this style is uncertain. They are mentioned in a Middleton bill of 1573, but if for Francis, he was beyond childhood by then.

> "For 1 yard dim of bayes to lyne my Mr. his cote and 2 pair cannyans 3s. 9d."

The codpiece continued to be made with trunk hose, but diminished in size after 1570 and disappeared in the 1590s. The close fit of hose was still maintained by material cut on the cross, but as knitting was becoming established in England during the second half of the sixteenth century, this method of construction was replacing the old.

> "For a payere of knitt hosez 6d. (for Francis) for a payre of garters 2d."
>
> 1550. (Middleton Accounts.)
>
> "For foure pounds of wooll for knittying hosen for my nepveu Fraunces 3s. 4d."
>
> (Ibid.)

The hose were attached to the doublet by "points" as in the fifteenth century.

Knee Breeches called *Venetians*, introduced about 1568 and lasting till 1620, might be fairly close-fitting or full and sometimes pear-shaped. Some were very voluminous and then called Venetian Slops. They were gartered below the knee.

> "Venetian hosen, they reach beneath the knee to the gartering place of the legge, where they are tied finely with silke points or some such like."
>
> 1583. (Philip Stubbes, *Anatomie of Abuses*.)

The codpiece was discarded and the front closure was made by buttons or ties which were hidden by the folds of the material.

Garters were small sashes tied on below the knee with the bow on the outer side and worn as a form of decoration rather than serving a useful purpose.

"For a payre of garters 2d." (for Francis).

1550. (Middleton Accounts.)

Children's shoes in the main followed the styles of their day. They were close-fitting up to the ankle and slashing was a favourite form of decoration. The broad square toe continued until *c.* 1540 when a rounded shape came into fashion. Heels were flat. Raised heels were not introduced before *c.* 1600. The commonest materials for shoes were leather and velvet, but silk and cloth were also used. Most shoes were lined.

"For a pair of lyned shoes for Mr. John Petre 6d."

1556. (Petre Accounts.)

Shoes for "Bairnes 1/6d, they being of sexteen year alld and if they be of less age non twelf yeirs auld the schone for sic bairnes be sauld for xiid."

1578–9. (Accounts of the Lord High Treasurer of Scotland.)

Note: The Scottish pound was equal to 1*s.* 3*d.* of English money before the Act of Union in 1707.

Out of doors *cloaks* were worn and were extremely fashionable from 1545 to 1600. The shape was circular, cut from about three-quarters of a circle. The length varied, as did the material which might be

"of cloth, silk, velvet taffeta . . . of dyverse and sundry colours, white, red tawine, black, greene, yellowe, russet, purple, violet. . . ."

1583. (Stubbes, *Anatomie of Abuses*.)

"For 5 yerdes of fryzado for 2 clokes and 2 cotes for the 2 boys at 10s. the yerde."

1556. (Petre Accounts.)

Cloaks were often edged with decorative bands or lace and with adults were tied at the neck with tasselled cords, but with children they appear to have been buttoned down the front.

"For a yerd and a halffe of lace for Johans'* cloke and a doussen of buttons 3d."

1556–7. (Petre Accounts.)

* John was 7 years old.

On the head boys wore caps and sometimes hats.

The most popular cap, sometimes called a bonnet, was a round cap with a narrow close upturned brim, and trimmed with a feather. It was worn perched on top of the head. The other style was known as a *flat cap* which had a flat mushroom-shaped crown spreading over a narrow brim and also trimmed with a feather.

"For two clothe cappes for the twoe younge gentlemen 2s. 8d."

1556–7. (Petre Accounts.)

"Item for a velvett cappe 10s."

1556. (Petre Accounts.)

Hats varied in shape quite considerably, especially during the second half of the century. They had moderately high crowns and narrow brims. They were made of felt or taffeta.

"For 2 hattes of taffita for them (young boys) 2s. 8d."

1557. (Petre Accounts.)

Taffeta hats were often called "Taffeta Pipkins" or merely "Pipkins". It was a small hat with a round crown pleated into a narrow flat brim and usually having a narrow jewelled hat band and feather trimming.

"For a felte hatte for worke dayes 2s."

1556. (Middleton Accounts.)

This felt hat was for Francis to wear at school.

The *hat band* was a most important item and was often of goldsmith's work for the aristocracy. The more usual material was cyprus, also spelt cipres and sepers. It might be either smooth or crimped like crêpe.

Night-caps were also worn by boys.

"For a blacke velvett night cappe for my nepveu Fraunces 3s."

1551. (Middleton Accounts.)

"For a sattyn nyght cappe for Gorge Farmer 22d."

1556–7. (Schoolboy friend about 7 and 8 years.) (Petre Accounts.)

Boys' shirts varied in quality,

"For three elles of holland for shyrtes (for Fraunces) 4s. 3d." 1550.

and later

C.C.E.–D

"for too elles of lynnen clothe and a halfe to make Mr. Fraunces shyrtes 3s. 9d."

> 1552. (Middleton Accounts.)

Shirts and also ruffs were starched.

"for a boxe of starche for my Mr. his shertes 8s. 6d."

> 1573. (Middleton Accounts.)

Gloves were worn by both sexes.

"For three payere of glovez for the chyldren 5d."

> 1550. (Middleton Accounts.)

Upper class boys when dressed in their best, might carry *rapiers* and *daggers*.

"For Mr. Frances to geve Hughe Hall for sending hym a dagger 6d."

> 1552. (Ibid.)

The following list comprises a suit of clothes for a kitchen boy:

"A paire of knit hose . . . 10d.
A paire of shewes 13d. . . .
For makinge a jerkin, dublet and breeches for the kitchen boye 16d."

> 1573. (Ibid.)

"To John Kemp, the boy of my Master's kitchen, an old hat, a black cap, two pairs of hand ruffs."

> 1582. (Will of William Markaunt of St. Giles, Colchester. E.R.O.)

Here are further extracts from that delightful book *The Elizabethan Home*, discovered in two Dialogues by Claudius Hollyband and Peter Erondell and edited by M. St. Clare Byrne. These dialogues are so descriptive of the Elizabethan schoolboy and his clothes that they deserve to be quoted fairly fully.

Dialogues from Hollyband:

(1) Getting up in the morning:
(Francis the schoolboy, a late riser; Margaret, the maid.)
"MARGARET: Ho Fraunces, rise and get you to school: you shall be beaten, for it is past seven: make yourself readie quiclly, say your prayers, then you shall have your breakfast.

FRANCIS: Margerite, geeve me my hosen: dispatche I pray you: where is my doublet? bryng my garters, and my shooes: geeve mee that shooyng horne.

MARGARET: Take first a cleane shirte, for yours is fowle.

FRANCIS: Make hast then, for I doo tarie too long.

MARGARET: It is moyst yet, tarry a little that I may drie it by the fier.

FRANCIS: I had rather thou shouldst be shent, than I should be either chid or beaten: where have you layde my girdle and my inck-horne? Where is my gyrkin (jerkin) of Spanish leather of Bouffe? Where be my sockes of linnen, of wollen, of clothe? Where is my cap, my hat, my coate, my cloake, my kaipe, (cape or short cloak) my gowne, my gloves, my mittayns, (mittens) my pumpes, my moyles (mules) my slippers, my handkerchief, my pointes, my sachell, my penknife and my books. Where is all my geare? I have nothing ready: I will tell my father. . . ."

1568.

The boy's *mittens* were gloves with a single compartment for the fingers and one for the thumb. The palm sometimes had a horizontal slit to allow the fingers to emerge without having to remove the whole mitten.

Pumps had soft uppers, usually of Spanish leather. Dancing pumps were worn by children. The mule was a slipper without heel-piece or quarter. The points were ties tipped with ornamental metal tags called aglets or aiglets. They were functional when used to attach hose to doublet as in "trussing the points" or ornamental when used in bunches or separately to decorate a garment.

In Dialogue 3, a naughty boy is about to be birched:

"MASTER: . . . Come hether companion, untrusse you: untie you, put your hosen downe, dispatche."

Dialogue 6 gives a picture of how the boys of noble birth should dress when going out with their mother. Guy and Rene are the boys.

"THE LADY (*to Guy her son*): You have almost atteyned to the age of nyne yeares, at least to eight and a halfe, and seeing that you knowe your dutie. . . . Think not that the nobilitie of your ancesters doth free you to do all that you list, contrarywise, it bindeth you more to followe vertue. . . . Come hether both of you, doe you weare your cloathes Gentle-men like?

Where is your hat-band? And where is the cipres of yours? Have you taken cleane shirts this morning? Your bands (collars) be not cleane.

Why have you taken your waste coates? (Under doublets worn for warmth.) Is it so colde? Button your dublet, are you not ashamed to be so untrussed? Where is your Jerkin? for this morning is somewhat colde: and you also, take your coate, are you ungirt? Boy (*the servant*) . . . goe fetch your Masters silver hatched Daggers, you have not brushed their breeches. Bring the brushes and brush them before me, Lord God how dustie they are! They are full of dust, what stockins have you? Your silke stockins or your worsted hose? Put on your garters embroidered with silver, for it may be that yee shall goe foorth with me. Where are your Cuffes and your falles? (Flat turn-down collars, often called falling bands.) Have you cleane handkerchers? Take your perfumed gloves that are lyned. Put on your gownes untill we go and then you shall take your cloakes lyned with Taffata, and your Rapiers with silver hiltes. Tye your shooe-strings. Well take your boot-hosen, and your gilt-spurres." 1568.

The rapier was now largely replacing the sword for gentlemen. It was slung from the belt by a hanger of goldsmith's work or an embroidered band.

Boot hose were stockings worn inside boots to protect the ordinary but more elegant stockings from dirt and wear. Boot hose were usually of coarse material, but some were "of the finest cloth that may be got". 1583. (Stubbes, *Anatomie of Abuses*.)

. . .

Little girls up to the age of 7 or 8 wore ground-length gowns composed of petticoat (i.e. skirt) and bodice, known as the body. These were not necessarily of the same material and the sleeves were sometimes detachable, the ties at the shoulder being hidden by wings. *Aprons*, with or without bibs, were worn by the younger children. A frill at the neck and wrist or a turn-down collar and cuffs or a

Girl, aged 20 months, wearing a gown
unmatching sleeves, probably detachable
under the wings. Apron with bib and
matching falling band, i.e. turn-down
collar. On her head a coif under a small
Mary Stuart hood. She holds a rattle with
bells and coral tip. 1572. (Longleat.
Daughter of the builder, Sir John Thynne.
Attributed to H. Eworth.)

lace-edged décolletage was worn, and usually not until they reached
their teens did they have to put up with the discomfort of ruffs which
came into fashion in the 1550s. There were exceptions of course.

> "For three quarters of red brode cloth for a petycote for my nece 5s.
> for halfe a yearde of redde russell for upper bodyez for the same,
> 8d."

1550. (Middleton Accounts.)

Boy aged 6 months in long gown and
apron. Winged sleeves, tall bonnet.
He holds a rattle with bells and tipped
with a stick of coral. 1564. (Son of Sir
John Thynne, builder of Longleat.
Attributed to Eworth.)

"For a yarde and halffe a quarter of Red sattyn of bryge (Bruges) for the upper body of Tomassyn* 2 petticotes 2s. 7d."

1556–7. (Petre Accounts.)

"Item for makyng of a peticote for Crystyan 9d, for makyng of a payr of fustyan sleves for hyr 3d." (i.e. detachable sleeves).

1556. (Petre Accounts.)

Older girls were dressed like their mothers. Their dress consisted of a *gown* and *kirtle*, the kirtle, after 1545, being the skirt portion and now not a whole garment. Sometimes the gown skirt would have a ∧ shaped opening in front revealing an embroidered under kirtle or a panel called a *forepart*.

"For mendyng of a gowne and a kyrtell of elesbethe Petre† and for sylke for the same 12d."

1556. (Petre Accounts.)

Both gowns and kirtles might be of very rich materials:

"For makynge a damaske gowne (for Margaret) 6s. . . . for makyng a payre of slevez and styching sylke 8d. . . ."

1556. (Middleton Accounts.)

"For a piece of blacke buckeram contaynyng 15 yardes for the chyldren gowns 10s. 6d."

1556. (Petre Accounts.)

Other materials used were cloth, taffeta, sack-cloth, damask and satin.

"Pd. for halffe an ownse of lace and for lyning the upper parts of elsabeth Petre's gowne of sattyn 13d."

1556. (Ibid.)

Kirtles were made of russell, (a Norwich worsted) velvet, and damask and consequently had to last. If the child grew the kirtle had to be lengthened to the ankles.

"For Satten of Brydyez (Bruges) to lett downe hir (Margaret's) crymsen damaske Kyrtell 20d."

1554. (Middleton Accounts.)

* Aged 13.
† Aged about 16.

Barbara Gamage and children. Centre, William unbreached and wearing a double-skirted doublet. Robert, the baby, aged 1. The little girls with aprons, the older girls in frounced farthingale skirts, bodices with pointed stomachers, cannon sleeves, open ruffs and adult hair styles, with billiments. 1596. (Painted 1596 by M. Gheeraerts. Penshurst Place, Lord de L'Isle and Dudley.)

Previous to *c*. 1545 the kirtle was filled out by under-petticoats. After this date the *farthingale* was introduced. This was a form of petticoat distended by hoops made of rushes, wood, wire or whalebone. The exact shape varied. The farthingale was covered with a variety of materials, some very expensive. Buckram, russet fustian and "for 4 yeardes and dim of redde russell for a vardingale 7s. 1d." 1551. (Middleton Accounts.)

Again:

"For 7 yardes of crimson sattin at 13s. the yarde for a Dutche gowne for Mistress Suzan £4. 11s. For a varthingale of mockado (imitation velvet) for her 7s."

1561. (Household Accounts of Richard Bertie Esq. and Lady Katherine Duchess of Suffolk, his wife.)

The bodice of most farthingale gowns at this period dipped to a sharp point at the waist in front, but the Dutch gown had a round waist. The wheel farthingale carried the skirt out horizontally from the waist, with a slight upward tilt at the back. The hard line produced at the circumference where the skirt fell vertically to the ground was usually hidden by a *frounced farthingale skirt* which had a gathered flounce projecting over the wheel. The girl's gown might have a high neck line finished with a circular ruff or the neck might be décolletee in front and worn with a fan-shaped ruff. "A payer of ruffs" indicated deep frills at the wrists.

"For loome lase to make Mistris Margaret . . . a payer of ruffez."
1554. (Middleton Accounts.)

Little girl aged 5 years, wearing a gown with cannon sleeves and wings, a circular ruff and an ornamental hood on her head. 1590. (Miniature by Isaac Oliver, Victoria and Albert Museum.)

The *Stomacher* was a long decorative panel, triangular in form, the point ending at just below waist level in front. It was worn with low-necked gowns in the second half of the century.

Girdles were usual but not essential.

"Item payd . . . for hyr 2 black gyrdels 8d."
1556. (Petre Accounts.)

It is interesting to note that little girls frequently had a book suspended from the girdle.

"for a boke for my cosen Margaret covered with velvett to hange at her gerdell".

1550. (Middleton Accounts.)

"for 14 yerdes of Reband of dyvers colors for gyrdels for my daughters and for Rebandes to hange there bokes (books) bye 4s. 6d.".

1556. (Petre Accounts.)

In some low-necked gowns the décolletage was filled in by a *partlet*. This was usually very decorative and made with a stand-collar, sometimes fastened by a clasp.

"For a claspe for Katheryne Petre* partelett 2d. For lace made with blacke and golde for a partelette for hyr" (Tomassyn).

1556. (Ibid.)

The word *kerchief* or *kercher* usually implied a neckerchief which was draped round the neck or over the head. The kercher might be edged with lace or a frill.

"For too elles of lynnen at 4s. th'ell for frose† cherchers."

1552. (Middleton Accounts.)

Handkerchiefs often meant neck wear also, in this century, but it was sometimes used in the modern sense, replacing the muckinder for older girls.

"For 2 doussen yerdes of lace to egge (edge) handkerchers after 12d. the doussen."

1556. (Petre Accounts.)

Whether these handkerchiefs were kept in their pockets is doubt-ful. *Pockets* were separate items, being flat pouches of linen slung from the waist beneath the skirt of the gown and reached through a placket hole.

"For a pocket for her gowne 2d." (Tomassyn's, aged 8.)

1553. (Petre Accounts.)

Gown sleeves were single or double. The single sleeves, wide and

* Aged 10.
† Frose probably means quilted or crimped.

loose and closed at the wrist, were worn by little girls. After 1575 older girls might have cannon or trunk sleeves. These were supposed to be the shape of a cannon and were made rigid with padding or distended with whalebone or reed, sewn into a lining of holland or fustian.

> "For makyng a payr of fustian sleves . . . 3d."
>
> 1556. (Ibid.) These would be for linings.

Some sleeves were knitted.

> "For knytting a payre of slevez 4d" (for Margaret).
>
> 1552. (Middleton Accounts.)

Double sleeves were tight at the shoulder, soon expanding into enormously wide hanging apertures from the elbow, whence a highly decorative undersleeve emerged to end at the wrist. This undersleeve generally had the back seam open at intervals as well as short vertical slashes, and through the gaps decorative material was "pulled out".

> "Payd for halffe a yerde of buckeram, a yerde of cotton, an ownse of sylke, 2 yerdes of poyntinge Reband and sarsenett for the pullying oute of the sleves in all 4s. 6d."
>
> 1556. (Petre Accounts.)

The girl's *night gown* was not, as implied, one worn at night or in bed. It was a loose unboned gown worn for warmth and comfort, both indoors and out, and was often very elaborate. Katherine Petre's (aged 10) was trimmed with fur.

> "For furrying of hyr night gowne 10d."
>
> 1556. (Petre Accounts.)

On the head, indoors, little girls wore coifs. From 1500 to about 1530, older girls might wear a plain draped hood, the material falling behind to the shoulders but having two straight lappets, generally embroidered falling down in front on either side. Noble ladies would wear a coronet over this. But from about 1520, some kind of head ornament or a *French hood* was usual. This was a small stiff bonnet placed far back on the head and showing much of the hair. The front border curved forward over the ears. This border was edged with a stiff ruched trimming called a "frose paste" and behind this curving round the hood, was the *nether billiment*, while arching over the crown farther back was the *upper billiment*. Both these were made of goldsmith's work and could be worn as separate head ornaments. The French hood had a hanging curtain behind.

> "Item payd . . . for 3 nether bylements for my 3 dawghters after 3s. the pece 9s. Payd for an upper bylement for tomassyn 4s. Item for makyng of 3 frenche hodes for my 3 daughters and for the makyng of one for myselffe after 12d. ye pece 4s."
>
> 1556. (Ibid.)
>
> "For makying of 2 hoddes 2s. and for Sattyn of one hoddes 16d."
>
> (Ibid.)
>
> "For makying Mris Margaret's Whoode, abylamentes and muffelers 3s. 8d."
>
> 1554. (Middleton Accounts.)

Little girl aged *c.* 5 years. Waisted gown, full sleeves with double wings. Falling band at neck. Billiment head dress. *c.* 1580. (Portrait of Arabella Stuart at Hardwick Hall.)

The *muffler* was a large square of material, folded diagonally and tied over the chin and mouth being knotted behind the neck. It is surprising to find this listed for a young girl, as its purpose for adults appears to have been to disguise. Probably in the child's case it was to protect her from breathing in cold air—or was it to stop her from talking? The curtain of the French hood when stiffened was sometimes turned up and worn flat on the head, supposedly to protect the complexion from the weather. It was then called a '*bongrace*'. This bongrace was also supplied as a separate article and was fashionable all through the century and into the seventeenth.

"For a bongrace for her (Mris Margaret) 5s. 8d."

1554. (Ibid.)

A less formal head wear for girls was the *caul*, which was a trellis-work coif or skull cap made of silk thread or goldsmithry and often lined with a coloured silk.

"Paid for a cawle of gold worke for Mistress Susan 45s."

1561. (R. Bertie Accounts.)

"Item for 2 calles (cauls) for Katherine Petre 7d. for herre (hair) laces for hyr 8d."

1556. (Petre Accounts.)

The *hair-laces* were decorative ribbons for binding the hair, which with young girls was allowed to flow loose.

The *voluper* was a beribboned head dress, also worn by young girls.

"For a hede lace and veluper for Mris Margaret 12d."

1552. (Middleton Accounts.)

Out of doors cloaks or cassocks were worn. The cloak was in the form of a three-quarter length cape.

"For makying a clooke garded with velvett 16d. for sylcke to the same 4d."

1551. (Ibid.)

Guards were decorative bands of some rich material used as borders and also to cover seams. The *cassock* was a long loose over-coat, buttoned down the front and sometimes made with cape collars.

"Item for furrying a cassocke of clothe for tomassyn 20d."

1555. (Petre Accounts.)

Mantles were trailing ceremonial cloaks fastened by long silk tasselled cords.

Hats from *c.* 1560s, with tall crowns and varying brims with or without an under cap or coif, were worn by their mothers, so presumably, when recorded, similar styles were worn by the daughters.

"for a hatt for Katherine Petre★ 5s."

1556. (Petre Accounts.)

Gloves were worn out of doors.

"For a payr of furred gloves (for Tomassyn) 3d."

1556. (Ibid.)

Girls' *shoes* were shaped like those of their brothers but played a relatively unimportant part in their wardrobe since they were largely concealed by their skirts. The materials varied.

"for makying 2 payr of showes for elsebeth Petre† 14d. Item for makying of 2 payr of fustyan of naples 20d."

1556. (Petre Accounts.)

"For 2 payr of showes, the one payr of fustyan of naples, the other of lether 17d."

1556. (Ibid.)

Their *stockings* or hose were either knitted or tailored.

"For 8 payer of knitt hose for the children 3s. 4d."

1561. (R. Bertie Accounts.)

Tailored stockings were chiefly made of Kersey, a fine twilled woollen cloth; sometimes of frieze, a napped woollen cloth.

"For an ell of carsey to make my nece hossen, 4s. 4d."

1550. (Middleton Accounts.)

"For a payr of freze hose for tomassyn 14d."

1550. (Petre Accounts.)

Garters were worn by little girls, in the form of ribbon or lace ties, bound above or below the knee.

"For 4 yerdes of lace for garters for tomassyn 3d."

1556. (Petre Accounts.)

★ Aged 10.
† Aged about 16. Fustian of Naples was a kind of mock velvet.

Two boys in doublets, bombasted trunk hose and wearing sash garters. 1575. (Detail from George Turberville's *The Booke of Hunting*.)

THE SEVENTEENTH CENTURY

Superstitions connected with child-birth and babies were still plenti-
ful. One which foretold sex appeal is mentioned in an old play of
1607.

"Indeed Miss, I believe you were wrapped in your Mother's smock,
you are so well beloved."

Thus wrapped at birth, the child would be specially attractive to
the opposite sex. However, following this temporary garment, if
worn, the child was swaddled. The *bearing-cloth* was the cloth in
which the child was carried to church to be baptised. It was usually
very ornate and used by the aristocracy.

New born baby in mantle. 1635–40.
(Detail from the Saltonstall Family, "The
Visit to the Bedside" by David des Granges.
Sir Kenneth Clark.)

"Here's a sight for thee; look thee,
A bearing cloth for a squire's child."

(Shakespeare—*A Winter's Tale*, Act III, Sc. 3.)

"For 5 yard of damaske to make a bearing cloth £3. 6. 6. For
Taffetie to lyne it 32s. For lace, eleven onceis to it 57s."

1623. (Lord Wm. Howard's Accounts.)

"Thy scarlet robes, as a child's bearing cloth. . . ."

(Shakespeare—*I Henry VI* Act I, Sc. 3.)

Cradle cloths too were often very ornate.

"For a read (red) flannel craddle cloth with goulde lace for Mr. Tho.
Howarde's childe 28s. 7d."

1629. (Howard Accounts.)

Baby caps were usually lace-edged.

"For lace capps for little Mr. Will Howard."

1629. (Ibid.)

Baby girl in long clothes. Bodice similar to her
mother's. The baby holds a coral and wears a
biggin. 1657. (Lady Fanshawe and her daughter
Mary by D. Teniers from a reproduction in *The
Memoirs of Lady Ann Fanshawe*.)

PLATE 3

Sir Walter Raleigh and his son aged 8 years. The boy in doublet, winged tight sleeves and very full Venetians, contrasting with his father's paned trunk hose and canions. The boy wears a falling band instead of a ruff. 1602.

Reproduced by courtesy of the National Portrait Gallery

PLATE 4

Little girl, aged 2, in dress with frounced farthingale skirt and sham hanging sleeves, her front hair brushed back over lace-edged cap. 1608.

Reproduced by kind permission of P. T. Mayston, Capetown

The *biggins* shaped like coifs were less ornate and generally warmer.

"3 yards of cloth to make biggins 6s. 6d."

1622. (Howard Accounts.)

The accompanying figure shows an actual set of baby's garments surviving from the seventeenth century. They are probably parts of a christening set. Other examples can be seen at the Gallery of English Costume, Manchester and elsewhere. They are often embroidered in the manner shown.

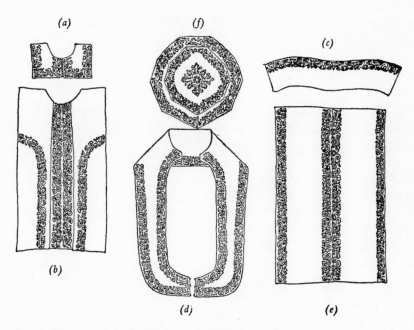

Baby garments, linen, embroidered with laid linen cord.
(*a*) Bib collar, probably worn over:
(*b*) Long bib.
(*c*) Head piece which was fastened under the chin beneath:
(*d*) The Stayband, worn with collar turned up over the head, the long ends pinned down over the long bib.
(*e*) A piece probably tied over the lower half of the body.
(*f*) A two-layered piece probably a pincushion cover.
(Nottingham Castle Museum, drawn by Zillah Halls.)

Baby clothes were sometimes made by their mothers as we gather from Mary Coke's letter to her husband in 1605.

> "I thank God that I can certify you that I am in health and comfort and do spend part of my time in making baby's clothes."

When swaddling was discarded, the child, at the age of 4 to 6 weeks old, was short-coated into a frock which just covered the feet. Charlotte de la Tremoille, a French lady married to the Earl of Derby, had very definite opinions on English habits.

> "I wish you could see the manner in which children are swaddled in this country (England). It is deplorable."
> January 1628. (*The Life Story of Ch. de la Tremoille Countess of Derby* by Mary Rowsell (London, 1905).)

(a)   (b)

(a) Boy aged 9 months in long frock, apron and bib, wears a decorative cap. 1663.
(b) Possibly his brother, aged 22 months, similarly dressed. 1663. (Possibly Walter and James Ogilvy, later 4th Earl of Findlater.)

"I have informed Madam of the baptism of your nephew. . . . He was carried by my sister-in-law and attended by the ladies of four gentlemen of rank of this country. I had him dressed in white after the French fashion, for here they dress them in colours, which I do not like."

April 1628. (Ibid.)

"As for our little one he is very well. . . . I have already in two of my letters asked you for frocks for him, for he is very big for his age; and they are needed the more that in this country children are short-clothed at a month or six weeks old. I am considered out of my senses that he is not yet short-coated. . . .
I also asked you to send hoods."

May 1628. (Ibid.)

Hoods and sometimes hats were worn out of doors over the indoor laced cap, as it was always considered essential to keep the head warm. In 1633, Doctor Chambers, in a letter to the King about the illness of his son, who had caught a cold, wrote:

Child in frock, apron and lace-edged cap.
Leading strings and rattle (bells and coral)
dangling over arm of chair. *c.* 1605.
(Douce Portfolio 136 (157) Bodleian
Library.)

"He stood late looking out at the bedchamber window, in the hands of one of his rockers, without either hat upon his head or neckcloth to his neck, which myself did see and reprove the rocker."

The rocker was a nurse hired to rock the cradle. However, Endymion Porter's letter to his wife, early in the century, advising her to let their eldest son, little George, play out of doors without a hat "else you will have him constantly sick" appears to have been followed. Certainly after breeching boys ceased to wear indoor caps and their hats were often carried in the hand. Little boys after being short-coated, continued to be dressed in frocks, with or without aprons, until the age of 6 or 7. At first they were indistinguishable from their sisters but usually by the time they were 5 years old,

Boy aged 1 year in frock with full skirt and lace-edged standing band at neck, with coif to match. Coral and bells hanging from neck. 1612. (Ancestor of the Hon. Andrew Shirley. Photo given by him.)

although the skirt portion called the petticoat was similar to that worn by little girls, the bodice portion was in the form of a doublet. This was buttoned down the front to waist level where a ribbon sash or narrow belt was worn. Sleeves were moderately full, and generally slashed or paned, and hanging sleeves real or false, the latter used as leading strings to control the child's efforts to walk, were almost invariably present.

PLATE 5

A queen and her son. She is holding his leading strings.
1610–15.

Reproduced by kind permission of the Trustees of the British Museum

PLATE 6

Little girl in tight bodice, winged sleeves and leading strings, frounced farthingale skirt, lace edged apron and bib, also coif. Compound ruff, cuffs at wrist. She holds a rattle with bells and coral. 1611.

Temple Newsam House, Leeds
Reproduced by kind permission of Captain V. M. Wombwell

At the neck ruffs were worn until the 1630s when wide lace-edged collars, known as falling bands, with matching cuffs, came into fashion.

Small boy in frock and apron with bib. Fashionable virago sleeves. He wears a lace-edged bonnet over a coif and holds a stick of coral. *c.* 1628–30. (Attributed to George Jamesone.)

"Looking on the lines of my boy's face, me thought I did recoil twenty three years, and saw myself unbreeched, in my green velvet coat, my dagger muzzled, lest it should bite its master, and so prove as armaments oft do, too dangerous."

1611. (Shakespeare—*A Winter's Tale*, Act I, Sc. 2.)

Breeching of the small boy at the age of 5, 6 or 7 was quite an occasion. In 1641 Sir Henry Slingsby wrote:

"I sent from London against Easter a suite of cloaths for my son Thomas, being ye first breeches and doublet yt he ever had, but yt his mother had a desire to see him in ym how proper a man he would be."

(*Diary* of Sir Henry Slingsby.)

And in 1679, Lady Anne North described the breeching of little Frank aged 6 years thus:

"You cannot believe the great concerne that was in the whole family here last Wednesday, it being the day that the taylor was to helpe to dress little Frank in his breeches in order to the making an everyday suit by it. Never had any bride that was to be drest upon her wedding night more hands about her, some the legs, and some the arms, the taylor butt'ning, and others putting on the sword, and so many lookers on that had I not a finger amongst them I could not have seen him.

When he was quite dreste, he acted his part as well as any of them, for he desired . . . to tell the gentleman (a schoolboy) when he came from school that here was a gallant with very fine clothes and a sword . . . there was great contrivings while he was dressing who should have the first salute . . . he gave it to me to quiet them all.

They are very fitt, everything, and he looks taller and prettyer than in his coats (petticoats). . . . I went to Bury and bo't everything

Boy, aged 6, in doublet with added false hanging sleeves and wearing a long petticoat. A muckinder suspended from waist. Fashionable broad falling band and lace-trimmed coif. 1632. (William 4th Lord Petre, Ingatestone Hall, Essex.)

for another suitt which will be finisht upon Saturday, so the coats (petticoats) are to be quite left off upon Sunday. . . . When he was drest, he asked Buckle whether muffs were out of fashion because they had not sent him one."

1679. (*The Lives of the Norths*, quoted by E. Godfrey.)

Boy, aged 5 years, in doublet with matching skirt (called a petticoat) open showing decorative underpetticoat a fashion of the day for women. He holds a large hat. 1630. (Christchurch Mansion, Ipswich.)

Muffs were not out of fashion for men at this time but perhaps little Frank was too young to have one. In the wardrobe account of Prince Henry, aged 14 years (the eldest son of James I) two muffs are listed.

"Embroidering two muffs viz. one of cloth of silver . . . the other of black satten embroidered with black silk and bugles."

1608. (See *Archaeologia*, Vol. XI, 1794.)

And again we find in a Scottish account book

"To my sone Wm. to buy a muff and gimsole £14. 2. 0."

1689 (Foalis Accounts.)

The *gimsole* was the same as *gamashe*, a high boot worn as a protection against dirt.

Three boys aged from left to right 9, 10, and 4 years.
All in doublets with wings to sleeves and falling ruffs
(fashionable from 1615 to 1640.) The two elder boys
are wearing full breeches "cloak-bag breeches", the
4 year old is still in petticoats. 1624. (Ian, James and
Patrick Campbell of Ardinglas.)

The boy's suit now consisted of a *doublet* and *breeches*. The doublet
went out of fashion in 1670 and the eighteenth-century coat style
began to take its place. Boys were always dressed in the fashion of
the day, but not invariably exactly like their fathers. Their doublets
followed the changing styles with short skirted squared tabs until
about 1610 after which the skirt was lengthened into deep squared
tabs or the tabbing might be absent. This style was worn until about
1645, but overlapping with it from the 1640s to 1670 was a loose
unwaisted doublet, the skirt being made up of a series of short
decorative tabs. Doublets were lined but not padded after 1630 but
bellypieces, that is triangular paste board stiffenings for the front
were sewn into the linings from 1620 to 1660s.

"Item bellypieces, stiffenings of buckram."
1625. (Tailor's bill, Coke Family Accounts. Cowper MSS. Com-
mission.)

Sleeves usually had wings until the 1640s, and during the 1620s
and 40s the front seam was often left open to show the shirt sleeve or
a contrasting lining and the body was often paned. With the waisted

PLATE 7

Small boy, aged 4 years. He wears a doublet with leading
strings attached, a full skirt called a petticoat and a lace-edged
coif and compound ruff. *c.* 1620.

Detail from a painting of Lady Apsley and her son
Reproduced by kind permission of Earl Bathhurst and the Royal Academy of
Arts, London

PLATE 8

Three youngest children of Charles I: James in long Spanish
hose trimmed with "fancies", bucket topped boots with frilled
boothose tops showing. Elizabeth in adult fashion with a neck
whisk. Henry is unbreeched. 1647.

Painting by Lely. Reproduced by kind permission of the National Trust

doublets narrow ribbon bands were worn and a series of ribbon bows, tipped with *aglets,* i.e. ornamental metal tags, was a common form of decoration round the waist. The doublet was fastened down the front by a close row of buttons or, more rarely, tied by "points", i.e. ribbons or laces tagged with aglets. Material used might be satin, velvet, and other costly stuffs. Less costly was canvas.

"6 dozen buttons for their dubbletts 18d
10 yards figurato at 4s and 8d for the 2 little gents 46s. 8d.
6 dozen buttons for the gents' dublets 18d."
1612. (The Household Books of Lord Wm. Howard, Surtees Soc., 1878.)

Small boy in doublet and open-fronted skirt. Sleeves with wings and hanging sleeves. He wears a broad falling ruff. 1628–32. (Lord Roos, son of the 6th Earl of Rutland, Botesford Church, Leicestershire. Figure on the monument of the Earl of Rutland. The boy was "killed by sorcery and evil practices".)

Figuretto was a costly flowered stuff thought to have been woven with metallic threads.

Prince Henry in 1608 had a:

"doublett and hose of greene satten cut and rased, cut out upon taffeta, lined with taffeta, the facing and pockets of taffeta, layed with silke lace, silke, stitching, and sewinge satten to collar".

and another:

"doublet and hose of narrow changeable watred silk grograine garled".

"3 yards of course canvyse 19d.
10 skeenes of silke 13d.
2 doz of pointes 10d."

1612. (Howard Accounts.)

Obviously the poor and their sons had doublets of very much cheaper material:

"A countrey fellow plaine in russet clad
His doublet mutton-taffety sheep-skins
His sleeve at hand button'd with two good pins."

1616. (S. Rowlands, *Doctor Merry-Man*.)

The *jerkin* or *jacket*, rarely called a coat, was worn over the doublet and followed the same pattern. It was now usually sleeveless having wings only. It appears to have been worn only by older boys and it went out of fashion completely by 1630 (except for the leather jerkin worn by men only and those worn by poor boys).

"6 poor boys to be taught to read, write and cast accounts; and to be provided with jerkins and breeches of grey frieze (the latter lined

William Sidney, aged 14–15, and Robert, aged 11–12. Both wearing fashionable doublets with short skirts in squared tabs, sleeves with wings, and knee breeches called Venetians. These are very wide and bombasted. Sash garters. *c.* 1605–6. (Painter unknown. Portrait at Penshurst Place, Kent, Lord de L'Isle and Dudley.)

with leather) stockings of blue yarn, and hats with watchet or blue bands."

15th August 1624.(Johnson's Charity, Lidlington, founded by Thos. Johnson, citizen and merchant tailor, London. Bedfordshire County Record Office, P. 196/2.)

One of Prince Henry's jerkins was "of black frizade" (a heavy worsted cloth similar to baize) "lined with shag", 1608, and he paid for "embroidering a jerkin and a pair of panes of perfumed leather, wrought about with gold, silver and coloured silk". The *panes* were long ribbon-like strips set close or produced by slashing, with the gaps revealing a coloured lining or the white shirt. These might be a decoration for the body or the sleeves. At the neck children wore either a turn-down collar called a falling band or a ruff. From 1615 when the falling ruff came into fashion, this was the style usually

Boy in short loose doublet worn open to show his shirt as also do his open sleeves. Small falling band showing tasselled band-strings (ties for fastening the collar). Shoulder belt for sword or rapier. Short Dutch breeches open at the knee (fashionable from 1600–1610 and again from 1640–1670s) trimmed with ribbon loops called "fancies". Wearing over-stockings usually worn with boots. Ribbon shoe strings. *c.* 1650. (By Wright, Collection of Sir John Hanbury Williams, Courtauld Institute.) An original suit of this date can be seen at the Victoria and Albert Museum.

given to children. It must have been slightly less uncomfortable for their short necks. Ruffs ceased to be worn after *c.* 1640. Lace-edged cuffs were usual at the wrist.

Leg wear was very varied. Trunk hose with canions were not worn by small boys, but presumably Prince Henry, aged 14, had a ceremonial pair since pockets are mentioned in connection with his hose. Trunk hose had vertical slits on either side for lined pockets. Trunk hose ceased to be fashionable, except ceremonially, after 1620. The three main styles of breeches for boys were:

(1) *Venetians* as already described—continued till about 1620.
(2) *Dutch breeches* (1600–10 and revived from 1640 to 1670s)—open at the knees and somewhat resembling modern shorts. From the 1640s they were often profusely trimmed with ribbon loops known as "*fancies*". They were buttoned down the front and later were provided with side pockets and fob pockets.
(3) *Cloak-bag breeches* worn in the 1620s and 30s were full and oval in shape, gathered in above the knee and there trimmed with ribbon loops or decorative "points".
(4) *Spanish Hose* (1630–45 and again 1660–70). These were high-waisted, long-legged breeches ending below the knees where they were either closed by ribbon bows or left open to overhang the stockings. The later styles were

> "buttoned up the sides from the knee with about 10 or 12 buttons".
> 1688. (R. Holme, *Academie of Armourie*.)

The earlier full breeches were distended with stiff linings, and

> "small furnishing, as Holland clothe, baies, canvas, rugg, bumbast, fustian and haire".
> 1608. (Prince Henry's Wardrobe.)

Small boys continued to truss their points until 1650, but older boys followed the new fashion. After 1630 until 1650 breeches were attached to the doublet, under the skirt, by large hooks and eyes and subsequently they hung round the hips without any fastenings.

Stockings were now usually knitted, in wool, cotton, thread or

Boy aged *c.* 15, wearing doublet trimmed
round waist with ribbon bows. A falling ruff
at his neck. His cloak bag breeches, oval and
ending above the knee, had just come into
fashion. Cloak round his arm and a large
beaver hat in his hand. Large "shoe roses"
fashionable from 1610–1680 and garters. *c.*
1620. (William, 3rd Earl of Lothian, Attributed to George Jamesone.)

silk, in various colours. Lady Brilliana Harley, however, wrote to
her son aged 15 thus:

> "Let your stokens be allways of the same culler of your cloths. . . . If
> your tuter does not intend to bye you silke stokens to weare with
> your silke sherte send me word, and I will, if plees God, bestow a
> peare on you."

1639. (*Letters of Lady Brilliana Harley, wife of Sir Robert Harley*, with

The HIGH BORNE PRINCE IAMES DVKE of YORKE
borne October the 13 1633

James, Duke of Yorke, aged *c.* 5 years. Doublet with slashed sleeves showing shirt sleeves. Doublet skirt made up of deep tabs. Long-legged breeches called Spanish hose. Stockings with lace-edged "tops": with adults these were always worn with boot-hose and called "boot hose tops". *c.* 1638. (British Museum, Catalogue of Engraved British Portraits. Engraver M. Merian.)

introduction and notes by Thomas Tayler Lewis, London, Camden Soc. 58, 1854.)
"For dying 3 pair of stockins for the gent 21d."
1612–13. (Howard Accounts.)
Stockings were gartered below the knee, the garters being decorative small silk sashes, which were tied in a bow on the outer side.

"Silk garters at 12s." 1608—belonged to Prince Henry.
"For 3 payre of silke garters 9s."
1633. (Howard Accounts.)

Stirrup hose were long stockings with an under-instep strap and no foot. They were worn over the silk stockings to protect them from dirt when on horseback, serving the same purpose as boot hose which

PLATE 9

Little girl, aged 8, in dress with basque bodice, "virago" sleeves and spreading lace collar called a "whisk". Feather head dress and fan. Skirt held up to show shoe-roses. 1632.

Attributed to Gilbert Jackson
Reproduced by permission of Shipley Art Gallery, Gateshead

PLATE 10

Children of Charles I: Charles (later II), Mary and James II.
Charles II, aged 4 years, unbreeched, wearing a night gown
and James II, aged 1 year, in doublet and petticoat. 1634.

A. Van Dyck
Reproduced by permission of Galleria Sabauda, Turin

were footed. Stirrup hose and boot hose were also worn by younger boys, quite apart from riding, as a protection to their fine stockings. These stirrup and boot hose frequently had a lace-edged frill at the top which was the only portion visible when worn with boots. These frills were known as boot-hose tops or merely "tops".

"A pair of stirrup-hose for Mr. Thomas". (Aged 16.)
1612–13. (Howard Accounts.)

On their feet boys wore *shoes* and *boots* similar in style to those worn by their fathers. The toe was rounded until about 1635. Subsequently it was square. Raised heels of leather or wood began to appear in 1600, the height increasing slightly through the century. The "little gent" in Lord Howard's Accounts evidently objected to raised heels.

"For takeing wooden heeles out of 4 payre of shooes of little Mr. Wm. Howarde 12d."

1633. (Howard Accounts.)

Shoes had open sides with ankle straps tied by ribbons arranged in decorative bows. Between 1610 and 1680 the bows were often

Boy of about 10, in high-waisted doublet with untabbed skirt, a fashion coming in after 1635. Decorated with ribbon loops down the front. Wearing Spanish hose and lace turn-down tops to stockings. Gauntlet gloves, large hat, sword and cane. *c.* 1635–40. (Attributed to Dobson. Collection of Lord Inchiquin, Dromoland Castle, Newmarket-on-Fergus, Co. Clare, Eire.)

C.C.E.–F

replaced by large rosettes of ribbon or lace, called *shoe roses*. Henry Peacham (the younger) when railing against the extravagant fashions of the time wrote:

"... and shoo-tyes that goe under the name of Roses, from thirty shillings to three, foure and five pounds the paire ..."

1638. (*The Truth of Our Times.*)

After 1680 the sides of the shoes were closed and the uppers ended in high squared tongues closed over by *buckles* or ties. *Pumps* were thin and soft, usually made of Spanish leather and worn by children for dancing.

Charles II, aged *c.* 11 years. Short doublet, Spanish hose unconfined at the knee. Sash garters tied in large rosettes. Large shoe roses. Short cloak, large hat. Small falling band at neck. Shoulder belt for sword. 1641. (Etching from a painting by Van Dyck, British Museum.)

"Pumps are shooes with single soles and no heels."

1688. (R. Holme, *Armourie*.)

They might be brightly coloured.

"3 pair of red dauncing pumps for the children 4s."

1612–13. (Howard Accounts.)

Boots were long and close-fitting, made of soft leather. Those with bucket tops were mainly worn on horseback. Prince Henry's boots were extremely luxurious:

"34 pair boots, faced with 13 yards satten of colours at 12/- and 3 yards velvet of colours . . ." 1608.

Brother and sister. Girl in gown typical of the period, and sham hanging sleeves. She wears a whisk round her decolletage. No cap but hair in the adult style. Her brother wears a short-waisted, short-skirted doublet and short sleeves without the front slit, loose short breeches trimmed with ribbon loops called fancies. He wears heavy jack-boots with square blocked toes and bucket tops, and large spur leathers. The lace-edged boot hose tops appear in the bucket tops. He carries a sugar-loaf hat. 1647. (Painter and sitters unknown. Photograph from *Country Life*.)

Prince Henry, aged 14, was also provided with *galoshes*, which in those days were wooden-soled low over-boots fastened by buckles. They were worn by all classes, though not with such buckles as were provided for Prince Henry:

> "Sixteen gold buckles with pendants and toungs to buckle a pair of golosses with gold." 1607–8.

Gamashes were worn by older boys either on horseback or as a protection against dirty roads when walking. They were high, close-fitting boots.

> "Gamashes, high boots, buskins or start-ups."
> 1688. (R. Holme, *Armourie*.)

Out of doors, cloaks of varying lengths and materials were the usual wear until about 1670. Cloaks were usually circular in cut and lined. They were often made to match the doublet and breeches. Again Prince Henry's are worth recording.

> "A cloake of green velvet, uncut, laid with green silke lace, lined with green satten, printed and rased in manner of embrod. and also an ell high with flowers, silke, stitching and sewing rebens and buckerame . . ." 1608.

Cloth was a common material and velvet a favourite lining.

On the head boys wore hats with large brims and moderately tall flat-topped crowns and as well as the hat band they were generally trimmed with a large feather or sometimes a bunch of ribbons. Hats were made of felt, shag, generally brightly coloured, velvet or silk, stiffened with buckram, or beaver. This last was the most popular until the 1660s and often a hat was simply called a "beaver". Prince Henry had

> "Beavers of divers colours, lined with sattin or taffata. . . . Plumes of feathers 40s, . . . embroidering an hat band with several sorts of pearls having set among the pearle, rubies, emrods and opals."
> 1608. (Prince Henry's Wardrobe.)

> "For one coolered hatt for little Mr. Wm. Howard 12s."
> 1633. (Howard Accounts.)

Boys' hair styles are not described in contemporary writings. They used hair powder in the 1640s and some began to wear wigs at that date.

> "I have sent you . . . some powder for your hair."
> 1642. (Letters of Lady Brilliana Harley.)

Portraits show that the hair was brushed back from the forehead and worn short until the 1630s when it was curled into the back of the neck and gradually worn longer, with a centre parting. Wigs began to appear towards the second half of the century.

> "Pray cutt off Tom's haire and sew it to his black cap, for I cannot gett a periwig under a peece for him."
> 1647. (*The Oxinden and Peyton Letters*, edited by Dorothy Gardiner, London, 1937.)

And in 1699 the Earl of Bristol paid £2. 3s. for a periwig for his son who was then under 8 years old.

Of *accessories*, gloves with gauntlet cuffs were worn by all boys out of doors.

> "6 pair of gloves for the children 2s."
> 1612–13. (Howard Accounts.)
> "Pd for a p. of gloves for little Willm Yeamans 3d."
> 1674. (Household Account Book of Sarah Fell of Swarthmoor Hall, edited by Norman Penny, F.S.A.)

Gloves were made of leather such as skins of sheep, lamb, stag, kid and doe. Cordovan, a Spanish leather, was very popular being fine and soft. Silk and worsted gloves were also worn. Perfumed gloves were very high class, and provided for Prince Henry.

> "One pair of gloves lined through with velvett and laid with three gold laces and gold fringe curled. Two pair of cordevant gloves, perfumed and laid with broad silver lace and fringe curled at 32s."
> "Six pair of plain gloves with coloured tops, being very well perfumed at 6s." 1608.

Rapiers were carried even by small boys of 8 or 9 until about 1650.

Daggers and swords were going out of fashion, but Prince Henry had all three in 1608.

Scarves took the place of the shoulder-belt for boys. They were worn diagonally from the right shoulder to the left hip for suspending sword or rapier.

> "For 2 ounces of gold lace to edge the child's scarf."
>
> 1625. (Coke MSS.)

Prince Frederick, aged 16, was given as a wedding present from his bride to be, Elizabeth of Bohemia,

> "a riche scarfe, embroidered all over upon carnation taffetas, both sides alike, with gold and silver and coloured silks and sundry devices; to have a sworde at".
>
> (*Elizabeth of Bohemia* by Carola Oman.)

The boy's wardrobe changed considerably after *c.* 1670 or a little earlier. The doublet went out of fashion and the *coat* took its place. This fell to the knees. It was slightly shaped in at the waist and had a back vent and two side vents from the hips, topped with hip buttons, and pleated. There was no collar, no lapels and the sleeves, at first elbow-length with a large turn-back cuff, reached nearly to the wrist by the end of the century. It was buttoned down the front from neck to hem. Under this was worn a *waistcoat* cut on similar lines and having sleeves, but no hip buttons or pleats. The *vest* was a term used in the 1660s and 70s for a loose waistcoat with elbow-length sleeves and sometimes girdled with a sash.

> "Pd . . . for buttens, silke and for makeinge a vest for little Willy Yeamans 3s."
>
> 1674. (Sarah Fell's Account Book.)

The under waistcoat was an undergarment worn for warmth.

> "for wt flannell for little Willm an under wast coate 1s 6d."
>
> 1678. (Ibid.)

The other change that took place towards the end of the century, in 1690, was the introduction of the three-cornered cocked hat.

Boys' *underclothes*, such as shirts and drawers, varied in quality according to the status of the wearer. Fine shirts and drawers were made of linen, or fine holland. Little Willy Yeamans had drawers made of "white ffustian", 1674 (Sarah Fell), but the cook's boy had:

"For 2½ yards of teare of hemp cloth for a shirt . . . at 12d per yard 2s 6d."

1674. (Ibid.)

It is noticeable that the colour blue is not mentioned in the description of any clothing during this century. Detailed records of children's clothes are only found among the upper classes and blue was a colour generally assigned to apprentices and serving men, hence the omission.

(a)   (b)

(a) Boy in doublet and petticoat. The doublet is long-skirted following the fashion. Sleeves slashed having wings and hanging sleeves. He holds a fashionable hat and gloves. 1628. (Part of a Triptych, Victoria and Albert Museum.)

(b) His sister in a long frock with sleeves and hanging sleeves like her brother's. She wears a lace-edged apron with bib and a decorative coif. 1628. (Part of a Triptych, Victoria and Albert Museum.)

In Henry Peacham's *Truth of Our Times* we find this:

> Of Parents and Children:
> (A father's Will) "To the third (son) . . . who came like a rogue in a foule shirt, and in a blew coat with one sleeve, his stockings out at the heeles, and his head full of straw and feathers. . . . I have nothing to beque-ath to you but the gallowes and a rope." 1638.

.   .   .

Little girls after being short-coated like their brothers, were dressed like their mothers and leather and whalebone bodices formed part of their wardrobes.

> "A pair of lether bodies for Mrs. Mary (aged 14) 3s. 8d."
> 1618. (Howard Accounts.)
> "Pd for sackcloth for a paire of bodies 3s.
> Pd for threed and bone for them 8d."
> 1631. (Executors Accounts, children of Thomas Hartley, 1624–39. L.C. R.O., W.C.W., 1640.)
> "The 28th was the first time the child (a little girl of three) put on a pair of whalebone bodice."
> 1617. (*Diary* of Lady Anne Clifford.)

The whalebone bodice could be the bodice of a gown stiffened with whalebone or a separate underbodice, as a pair of stays. These in the form of corsets were worn at the end of the century.

> "making a pair of stays £1. 10. 0."
> 1699. (Child aged 13.) (S. Tufnell of Langleys.)

The child's *gown* now consisted of a bodice called a "body" and skirt, called a "petticoat", often shortened to "coat". The petticoat was not an undergarment as in the nineteenth century, unless called an underpetticoat.

Children's gowns were fastened down the front by a close row of buttons, a series of ribbon bows or sometimes by lacing. The skirt or "petticoat" was expanded by stiffened underpetticoats or by the farthingale which went out of fashion in the 1620s.

> "For Canvis, whalebone and other things necessarie for makinge up a gowne for Mrs. Elizabeth Howard 6s. . . .
> For making . . . Elizabeth . . . a gowne and peticote."
>   1633. (Howard Accounts.)

The sleeves were close-fitting to the wrist and wings were usual until about 1640. In the 1620s the vertical slash, like that of their brothers, was popular. Subsequently sleeves grew wider and when ballooned and slashed were known as *virago sleeves*. Double sleeves were also worn in the 1630s. During the second half of the century sleeves became elbow-length and full. Some had cuffs, some widened to be finished with a frill or with the chemise flounce. With younger children hanging sleeves were sometimes present though after 1630 these were debased into long strips of material forming sham hanging sleeves and functioning as leading strings or left as ornaments when ceasing to be of use. They were sewn to the back of the arm-holes.

Young girl, aged *c.* 8, in dress with tight bodice, cannon sleeves and frounced farthingale skirt. Fan shaped standing band at neck and jewelled head ornament. *c.* 1604. (Elizabeth of Bohemia by ? M. Gheeraerts the younger. Lord North, Wroxton Abbey.)

"Women . . . when they are children, they fool their fathers; and when they have taken leaves of their hanging sleeves (leading strings) they fool their gallants."

1671. (Wycherley—*A Dancing Master*, Act V, Sc. 1.)

"Upon the 1st (May) I cut the child's strings (i.e. leading strings) off from her coats (i.e. dress) and made her use togs alone, so she had two or three falls at first but had no hurt with them."

1617. (*Diary* of Lady Anne Clifford.)

The child was 3 years old.

Little girl, aged 2 years, in gown with embroidered stomacher front and full sleeves open, showing smock sleeves. Full gathered skirt and apron without bib. Long sham hanging sleeves. Deep collar called a gorget, with matching cuffs. Large feather trimmed hat on table which would be worn over her coif. 1661. (Miss Campion, frontispiece to *The History of the Horn Book* by A. W. Tuer.)

"I find his daughter Betty that was in hanging sleeves but a month or two ago, and is a very little young child, married."

> 30th July 1663. (Samuel Pepys's *Diary*.)

"I did see the young Duchess (Princess Mary, afterwards Queen Mary) a little child in hanging sleeves, dance most finely."

> 2nd April 1669. (Ibid.)

The neck line varied. If closed high, a ruff might be worn until the 1640s.

"For making little Mrs. Eliza ruff 4d."

> 1622. (Howard Accounts.)

This ruff could be circular, falling or stand-fall, that is rising at the back of the neck. The oval ruff was a feminine fashion from 1625 to 1650. It spread laterally in formal tubular pleats or *sets*, as they were called, and was closed all round. It could only have been worn by older girls in their teens. The low-necked bodices having a square or rounded décolletage in front were worn with a fan-shaped ruff or collar which stood up round the back of the head. This was kept in place by a wire support called a *rebato*.

"A rebato wyer for Mrs. Mary 8d."

> 1612–13. (Howard Accounts.)

Girl, aged 9 years, in paned bodice, and sleeves with wings and "in a ruffe with a feather in her head". 1622. (Lady M. Fielding, daughter of the Earl Denbigh, later Duchess to the First Duke of Hamilton. National Galleries of Scotland.)

Others were finished with lace-edged falling collars known as *falling bands* or merely "falls" and in the second half of the century when these were deep and broad, they were known as *whisks.*

> "pd for a blacke allamode whiske for Sister Rachell 2s."
>
> 1677. (Sarah Fell's Account Book.)

Alamode was a thin light glossy black silk.

Lace-edged cuffs at the wrist were usual with long sleeves.

> "For 2 yards and a half of loom work to make Bess and Anna cuffs and falls."
>
> 1625. (Coke MSS.)

Waistcoats were close-fitting jacket bodices worn with a skirt

Little girl in long frock and apron with bib. Full sleeves and hanging sleeves and lace-edged falling collar called a whisk. The front hair swept back over her cap is a characteristic feature for small girls of this period. 1649. (Portrait dated by J. C. Meyern, Audley End.)

called a petticoat, being rather more comfortable than the whale-bone bodice. They were also worn at night for warmth.

> "For making wayscottes and mending clothes for his sisters, 2s."
>
> 1633. (Howard Accounts.)

The following is from a letter written by Mr. Ellwood in prison.

> "The chief thing I now wanted was employment . . . I got to work from a hosier in Cheapside; which was to make night waistcoats of red and yellow flannel for women and children."
>
> 1622. (*The Penns and Penningtons of the 17th Century* by Maria Webb.)

> ". . . 21 yards . . . will make 2 petticoats and waistcoats for my nieces Ursula (aged 15) and Cicely (younger), being allowed 6 breadths in the petticoats which will be near as full as my wife's. The taffeta is intended to line the sleeves and skirts of the waistcoats, which is also to serve for the trimming, it being turned over with an edge on the panel of the sleeves and skirts."
>
> 1631. (Sir Oliver Boteler to his nephew about clothes for his nieces Ursula and Cicely Taylor. From *Bedfordshire Letters of Bunyan's Day*, A. T. Gaydon and P. L. Hull, B.C.R.O., Leaflet No. 2.)

Night gowns as in the previous century were loose and comfortable and worn during any part of the day. They were often very ornate. Princess Elizabeth of Bohemia when she was 16 had two "night-gowns tissued very high in severall flowers". They were lined with carnation wrought satin. She also had a "Lappe Mantle and Cloake". The Lap-Mantle was a rug to cover the knees when travelling. The Princess's was of tawny two-pile velvet, fur-lined, and she had another of silvered velvet. (*Elizabeth of Bohemia* by Carola Oman.)

Materials for the children's gowns were: velvet, baize (a thin serge), taffeta, morelly (a kind of tabby), tabby (a coarse thick taffeta glossy and watered), silk, and "stuffe" (a worsted lacking nap or pile). In the following quotation the coat or petticoat includes the whole dress.

> "This day the child did put on her crimson velvet coat, laced with silver lace, which was the first velvet coat she ever had."
>
> 1619. (*Diary* of Lady Anne Clifford.)

"For a yard and a half of baize to make the child a petticoat."

1625. (Coke MSS.)

"For 12 yeardes of Philip and Cheyney and other thinges necessarie for a coate for Mrs. Marie Howard 29s. 8d."

1633. (Howard Accounts.)

Peg, aged 11 or 12, having very much annoyed her father, had to forgo having a gown of stuffe. Perhaps the colour did not suit her.

"I sent thee the newest and best fashion stuffe in London . . . for a gound (gown) and petticoate . . . for my two daughters; but since Peg is so refactorie lett her weare her old clothes; the stuffe is an excellent stuffe and much worne, though formerly in fashion."

1647. (*The Oxinden Letters—1642–70.*)

"My mother bought ye child a Morelly coate striped yellow and black."

1681. (*Verney Memoirs.*)

Yellow appears to have been a favourite colour in this century. Princess Elizabeth of Bohemia in 1601 when she was only 5 years old, was supplied with gowns of yellow satin of figured velvet, black upon red, of white satin upon carnation, of Spanish taffetas, trimmed with plush, of orange and popinjay* crêpe, with metal fringe round the neck. In winter she was clothed in warm purple serge and brown Spanish frieze. (*Elizabeth of Bohemia* by Carola Oman.) Black was worn for mourning and the Princess wore a black satin gown, brocaded with silver flowers, on the death of her brother Prince Henry in 1612.

Aprons were worn as elegant accessories to the costume and though usually white were sometimes coloured.

"For 13 yeardes of Scotts for aprons for little Mrs. Marie and Mrs. Elizabeth Howard 17s. 4d."

1629. (Howard Accounts.) ("Scots Cloth" was a linen woven from nettle fibres instead of hemp.)

* Green or blue.

"Pd for 3 blue aprons . . . for 2 yards of cobweb laces for Bess (the child)."

1625. (Coke MSS.)

On the other hand, aprons for domestic use were always part of a working girl's outfit.

"Ann Castleman (having finished her 'apprenticeship') shall leave . . . apparelled with two new gowns, two new petticoats, one paire of boddys (stays) two paire of stockings, one paire of shoes, two new shifts, two new aprons, one straw hatt, two suites of head cloathes and two handkerchiefes fitt . . . for such an apprentice."

1698. (B.C.R.O., D.D.P. 64/14.)

Indoor caps called coifs, shaped like a baby's bonnet, were always worn by little girls until they neared their teens when head ornaments similar to those worn by their mothers were allowed. The coifs were usually edged with lace or embroidered and made of linen or crewel, a worsted.

"I send you . . . for the children a cruel coife and . . ."

1620. (Coke MSS.)

Small boy aged 2 years and his sister, standing. Both wear aprons with bibs. He holds a coral stick. 1650. (Portrait by Mytens. Netherby Hall. Copyright to *Country Life.*)

With the coif a *cross cloth* was sometimes worn by older girls. This was a triangular piece of material with the straight border over the forehead and the point behind. It was either tied under the chin or at the back of the head.

"Pd for 2 cross clothes 1od.
Pd. for 2 coives 11s."
1634. (Executors Accounts, children of Thomas Hartley, 1624–39. L.C. R.O. W.C.W., 1640.)

From 1690 to 1710 the *fontange*, which was a French fashion, was worn on ceremonial occasions only by royal little girls. This had a close-fitting crown at the back of the head with a tall erection in front of lace or lace and linene frills kept upright by the *commode*

Child in go-cart. Frock, apron with pointed bib and leading strings and coif. 1650–60. (Norwich Castle Museum, artist unknown.)

PLATE 11

Three children of Charles I: Charles (later II), aged 5, now breeched, wearing fashionable doublet and Spanish hose fastened below the knee with sash garters tied in large rosettes. Large shoe roses and spreading falling band at neck, a style very fashionable in the 1630s. James, aged 2 years, still unbreeched. 1635.

A. Van Dyck
Reproduced by gracious permission of Her Majesty the Queen

PLATE 12

Lord Buckhurst, later 5th Earl Dorset, aged 15, in loose doublet, broad falling band typical of the 1630s. Wearing long Spanish hose closed below the knee with sash garters. Very large shoe roses fashionable from 1610–80. Cane in hand. Cloak under arm. His brother similarly dressed. 1637.

Cornelius de Neve
Reproduced by kind permission of Mr Lionel Sackville–West, Knole, Kent

which was a wired support. There were usually two long lace streamers called lappets hanging down behind. Hair-laces were worn as in the sixteenth century.

"For one hayre lace for litle Mrs. Marie 6d."

1629. (Howard Accounts.)

Hair styles were simple. The front hair was brushed straight back from the forehead and the back hair at first short to the neck, later fell in curls to the shoulders.

"Curling irons for Mrs. Mary 3s."

1618. (Howard Accounts.)

An occasional hair style for little girls during the first three-quarters of the seventeenth century was to brush back from the forehead, a central lock of hair over the coif, to be caught in at the back of the head.

Out of doors cloaks were worn and on the head soft hoods over the coif. In the seventeenth century these hoods were called *chaperones*.

As a protection for their complexion little girls were sometimes provided with *masks*. These covered the face being pierced opposite the eyes, nose and mouth. Some covered the upper part of the face only. They were usually made of velvet or satin. Princess Elizabeth had one at the age of 5 and Lady Anne Clifford bought herself one at the age of 10 in 1600.

"And for the children . . . 2 green masks."

1620. (Coke MSS.)

"For a velvit maske for her (Mrs. Marie) 16d."

1619. (Howard Accounts.)

Gloves were worn out of doors, and these were made of kid, thread or silk. They were often coloured and sometimes embroidered.

"For couleringe 3 p. of gloves for Sist. Rachel 6d."

1673. (Sarah Fell's Account Book.)

C.C.E.–G

"4 pear of kid gloves 4s. 4d.
2 pear of thred gloves 3s. 6d."
        1699, for Elizabeth Tufnell aged 13. (S. Tufnell of Langleys.)

Girls' *shoes* were similar to those worn by their brothers. They also wore dancing pumps. Their stockings were often brightly coloured. Lady Anne Clifford as a child of 10 had

"a pair of green stockings" *c.* 1600.

and

"pd for dieinge a p. of stockens sea greene for Sist. Rachell 4d. for dieinge 2 p. sky couler for Sist. Susannah 4d."

is recorded in Sarah Fell's Accounts in 1676.

Brother and Sister. Little girl in low-necked gown with full sleeves and leading strings. Long gathered apron. Front hair brushed back over cap as on page 92. Her brother in similar gown but wearing a falling band with tasselled band strings. *c.* 1662. (The Southcote children, Mary and Edward, Ingatestone Hall, Essex.)

Little girls also wore garters. These were small sashes of ribbon, worsted, crewel or list, i.e. tape. They were tied above or below the knee.

"Garters for Mrs. Mary 6d."

1612–13. (Howard Accounts.)

"When we were maids. . . .
Garters of list, but now of silk,
Some edged deep with gold. . . ."

1606. (Warner's *Albion's England*.)

Generally speaking, the fashions for young girls in this century gave "little ease". John Bulwer had very definite opinions on the subject.

"Another foolish affectation there is among young virgins though grown big enough to be wiser, but that they are led blindfold by custome to a Fashion pernitious beyond imagination; who thinking a Slender Waste a great beauty, strive all that they possibly can by streight-lacing themselves, to attain into a wand-like smalnesse of Waste, never thinking themselves fine enough untill they can span their Waste. By which deadly artifice they reduce their Breasts into such streights, that they soon purchase a stinking breath; and while they ignorently affect an august or narrow Breast, and to that end by strong compulsion shut up their Wastes in a whale-bone prison or little-ease, they open a door to consumptions, and a withering rottennesse."

1650. (*The Artificial Changling*.)

THE EIGHTEENTH CENTURY

THE EIGHTEENTH CENTURY

In the early eighteenth century babies were still *swaddled* at birth,

"Bought of Thomas Heckford . . . a swadling ban 7d."
1729. (Essex Record Office, D/DO.)

but the custom was dying out in England.

Pamela, in Richardson's novel, studies Mr. Locke's book (*Thoughts concerning Education*) and fervently agrees with his comments about young children being clothed too warmly and too tightly:

"How has my heart ached many and many a time when I have seen poor babies rolled and swathed, ten or a dozen times round; then blanket upon blanket, mantle upon that; its little neck pinned down to one posture; its head more than it frequently needs, triple-crowned like a young pope, with covering upon covering; its legs and arms as if to prevent that kindly stretching which we rather ought to promote . . . the former bundled up, the latter pinned down; and how the poor thing lies on the nurses lap, a miserable little pinioned captive."

In this strongly expressed opposition to swaddling babies, Pamela, or her author, is probably reflecting a current view, the new attitude towards swaddling which was soon to bring it to an end in England. That she should study Locke's work is a comment on the pervasive influence of his ideas at this period (1740–1) and at this level. It seems likely that the movement towards greater freedom in children's dress in this century owes more to Locke than to Rousseau. *Emile* was not published until 1762, when change was already evident in England, although one of Locke's particular ideas, that children should sleep bare-headed at night, took almost another hundred years to win acceptance. Another idea, that children should get their feet wet and keep them wet, has yet to be accepted, but Sophie von la Roche, visiting England in 1786, remarked on the bare feet of English babies:

"People, I noticed like to have their children with them and take them out into the air, and they wrap them up well, though their feet are always bare and sockless."

(*Sophie in London*, 1933.)

By 1785, a doctor writing in the *Lady's Magazine* could say, "The barbarous custom of swathing children like living mummies, is now almost universally laid aside." It had been laid aside long enough for him to say also, "As many of our fair readers may never have had access to know or see this process of swathing, formerly used almost universally over Europe, we shall here give a description of it . . ." and this is his account:

"As soon as the infant is well cleaned, he is wrapped up in his swaddling cloaths; they first put on a shirt slit open before, they afterwards gird the breast with a square piece of cloth, (called a bed) which extends even to the feet, over which they apply a woollen roller, three inches broad, in circles which extend obliquely, descending towards their inferior extremities, from whence they roll it back again to the waist. They also sometimes content themselves with taking some circular turns on the breast, and with keeping the arms stretched by means of pieces of linen, or a woollen waistcoat, put over the bed. Upon this the infant is laid, and its arms confined, and extended against its body by a fold made in this waistcoat, and the whole kept close by another woollen roller, of about two ells in length, applied in circles like the former. In short, over all they put a blanket, which is worn for a certain time in all seasons. In many places the infant thus swathed is laid upon a square mattress stuffed with feathers, one angle of which sustains the head, while the other answers to the feet; this last is doubled up and fastened to the two lateral corners with large pins.

As to the head it is covered with two or three small biggins, the first of which is of linen, and the others woollen, and these are tied behind the neck. In many places they add a stayband, or a kind of head dress with two ends which hang down on the side of the head, and are fastened on the breast with pins, in order to make the infant hold its head straight, which very well supplies the want of the mattress just mentioned."

In spite of their dangers pins were used a good deal in baby clothes.

Steele, in the *Tatler*, 1709, describes the sufferings of a new-born child:

> "The girl was very proud of the womanly employment of a nurse and took upon her to strip and dress me anew, because I made a noise, to see what ailed me; she did so and stuck a pin in every joint about me. I still cried; upon which she lays me on my face in her lap; and, to quiet me, fell a-nailing in all the pins, by clapping me on the back."

A linen *shirt* open down the front, usually made from a single piece of material seamed on the shoulders with openwork stitching or lace insertion, was worn beneath the swaddling bands and also when swaddling was abandoned. Baby shirts of the eighteenth century had a round or slightly squared neck, sleeves set in plain, or slightly gathered at the shoulder, with a gusset, and open or gathered into a band at the elbow. Neck and sleeves were often trimmed with narrow edgings of bobbin lace or frills of muslin. When the child left off swaddling bands, *stays* and a flannel petticoat were worn over the shirt. A very small pair of boned stays in the Victoria and Albert Museum may be evidence that babies wore a boned bodice, but the stays mentioned amongst their clothing, may often have been of stiff material, corded or quilted rather than boned. The clothing of Mary Brudenell, a baby of 1718, was listed as:

> "4 night pilches, 2 dozen and 10 damask clouts, a dozen diaper bibs, 5 short stays and 4 lace skull caps."
> (Account of Children's Linen and Plate, Brudenell MSS., quoted in *Brudenells of Deene*, J. Wake, 1953.)

Clouts are obviously napkins, and a *pilch*, then, as later, was a flannel cloth put on over the napkin at night,

> "flannel cloth to wrap about the lower part of young children".
> (*Ladies Dictionary*, 1694.)

Over stays and flannel petticoat, beneath the frock, there was often a linen or muslin *slip*, a straight piece of material with vertical tucking round the top to shape it to the body. In the *Benenden Letters* (1901), baby clothes of 1785 were listed, "muslin for three common frocks; long lawn for 1 doz shirts; cambric for six caps; calico for four or five bedgowns; flannel for three undercoats".

Childbed wear for the poor comprised shirts, caps and undercaps, made of long lawn; frocks of printed cotton (three yards made two frocks); squares of diaper; squares of flannel; and skirts made of figured diaper, each skirt having five 18-inch breadths in it, and a yard doubled down the middle for a band,

"the skirt plaited into the band, the most plaits before".
(*Instructions for Cutting Out Apparel for the Poor,* 1789.)

Caps were an important part of a baby's dress. They were worn from birth, both by day and by night. At the beginning of its life a child wore two, a plain close-fitting undercap and a cap. There might also be a separate headpiece, edged with a frill or lace to show beneath the cap. *Headpieces* survive in some numbers, some made in the shape of the front of the cap, others a triangle with lace on one side and tapes long enough to bring down to the chin, cross there and take up to the headpiece again. The caps themselves survive in a variety of shapes, but there are two main types: those made to fit the head closely, cut in three sections with the central one extending from the forehead to the neck; and those made with a caul, gathered into a front section or headpiece. The former includes most of the quilted caps or those of stiff linen made stiffer by embroidery. The latter are of fine linen or muslin and may have a headpiece in two layers or one; they may have a lace insertion down the centre of the headpiece, or down the centre of the caul; or they may have a small crown of lace in the caul with an insertion from it to the nape. Many of these insertions are worked in the needlepoint lace known as "holie-point". One, in the Gallery of English Costume, Manchester, made with the double headpiece and with a small crown and insertion of lace has the date "1744" worked in the needlepoint lace. The caps are often edged with lace or muslin frills.

The first frocks changed very little during the first half of the century. They had a round or square neck revealing the frilled edge of the shirt; the sleeves ended at the elbow, usually with a turn-back

cuff, with the frill of the shirt sleeve showing beneath. The bodice
was close-fitting, and the full skirt was seamed on to it at the waist.
Until the child started to walk, the skirt fell just below the feet. A
back opening was probably most general and sashes were worn.
During the second half of the century the neck grew lower and the
sash was worn higher, and then the bodice shortened and loosened.
Mrs. Papendiek's first child, Charlotte, was born in 1783. In 1784:

> "We made her four white frocks and two coloured ones with the
> skirts full and three tucks and a hem; the bodies plain, cut crossways
> and the sleeves plain with a cuff turned up. . . . The rest of her attire,
> was long cotton or long thread mitts without fingers, tied round the
> arms high above the elbow; a double muslin handkerchief crossed
> and tied behind in a bow, or if cold, a silk pelerine with the same
> coloured bonnet, close front, high caul, a bow in front. Baby's was
> blue and very pretty she did look."
>
> (*Mrs. Papendiek's Journal, etc. Ed. by V. B. Broughton,* 1886.)

For the christening the child wore a special robe. A number of
these survive. The usual form is a robe of white satin, about a yard
long, open down the front, the bodice shaped by vertical tucks, with
bound shoulder straps and detachable sleeves. The opening is often
trimmed with silk braid and knotted fringe. Many of the sets of caps,
headpieces, bibs, sleeves and mittens which survive are probably
christening sets. A christening set appears in the Furnese accounts
in 1715; it cost £21.* A mantle might be worn over the robe
Susan Sibbald recalls her sister's christening in 1792:

> "Grace had laid out for the occasion a most beautiful blue and white
> satin mantle; blue hat and feathers, presents from Lady Paine, one
> of her Godmothers."
>
> (*Memoirs of Susan Sibbald,* 1783–1812, 1926.)

In the Victoria and Albert Museum there is a doll, dressed in a
complete set of baby clothes, in the style of the middle of the century.

---

* In the accounts kept by the wife of Sir Robert Furnese there is mention of a
white sarsnet hood being bought for her daughter (afterwards Marchioness of
Rockingham and later Duchess of Guilford), in 1714 when she was not more than
a year old. The christening set was probably for the son Harry who was born in
1715.

On its head are undercap, triangular headpiece and cap; it is wearing
shirt, napkin, two flannel and one linen petticoat, all three open down
the front; over these it has a silk robe, also open down the front, and
over this a long lace-trimmed bib, like those of many of the christening sets; there are mittens on its hands.

.   .   .

Children were short-coated when they were about a year old,
although in 1747, one girl, Mrs. Boscawen's daughter, was not short-
coated until she was 20 months old (*Admiral's Wife*, C. Aspinall-
Oglander, 1940). In 1784, Lady Grantham short-coated her youngest
son at 9 months, which from that time onwards was the usual age:

> "Your little boy [this appears to be Philip, born October, 1784] goes
> on very well and has just got shoes and short petticoats."
> (Letter to the Marchioness Grey, Beds. County Record Office,
> L/30/9/81.)

Boys continued to wear frocks up to the age of about 4. These
frocks resembled the frocks they had worn as babies, and the frocks
worn by their sisters, but now cut shorter so that the frock usually
cleared the instep, and the bodice was often separate from the skirt
or petticoat, particularly if it were boned. There is a *boned bodice* in
the Gallery of English Costume, Manchester, which by family

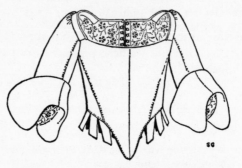

Boy's bodice, red wool, boned, 1725.
(Gallery of English Costume, Manchester.
Drawn by S. Gregory.)

tradition was worn by a boy in 1725, and in the portraits of the early eighteenth century, bodices of children of this age appear to be either stiffened themselves or worn over a stiff stay bodice. One of the clothed effigies in Westminster Abbey is of the little Marquess of Normanby, who died early in 1715, just after he was 3 years old. The effigy is fully dressed, probably in the child's own clothes which include a stay bodice* of yellow silk and linen, stiffened with cane, with shoulder straps tied with ribbon, and showing much the same shape as the bodice at Manchester. In the Furnese accounts (Guilford MSS., K.A.O.) there is an entry for 1722, "Making Kitty's coats and a pair of stays for Harry £3 1. o.", when Harry was about 6 or 7 years old.

Boys often wore long, front-fastening gowns, sometimes with a wrap-over front. The dress of the effigy is a gown with brocaded silk front and yellow silk back and sleeves with cuffs of the brocade; the front wraps over and is held in place by a sash. Over this is a full-length coat of red velvet, braided and frogged, but not quite meeting across the front. Both garments have slits behind the shoulders, presumably for leading strings.† This dress is very like that worn by one of the sons of the Earl of Morton in a painting by J. Davison, signed and dated 1740. Again Reynolds' painting of the Penn family of 1763–4 shows a 3- or 4-year-old boy wearing an open coat over a frock with broad sash. In York Castle Museum there is a garment of this kind in yellow and white striped silk, fastening to the waist, with slit cuff on the sleeve, probably from the second quarter of the century, and another example in blue silk at Ham House. The description in the *London Gazette* (4149/4) in 1705, of a missing boy, "James Smith . . . upwards of four years of age in a hanging sleeve coat and a painted frock", probably meant this combination of garments. The word *frock* was used for children's long-skirted dresses in general. It is noteworthy that from about 1730 the term frock was also used for the informal coat with turn-down collar, worn by men and boys. The word *coat*, until the end of the century, also had the

* Illustrated in F. Libron, *Le Corset . . .*, 1933.

† For the full description see *Archaeologia*, 1936. On Some Later Funeral Effigies in Westminster Abbey, L. E. Tanner and J. L. Nevinson.

meaning of petticoat or skirt. For a boy to be "in coats" meant that he was still wearing his long-skirted childish frocks:

> "he says then he was a naughty baby in coats, but now he is a man he's sure Papa won't whip him".
>
> (Admiral's Wife.)

The term *nightgown* also occurs in the first half of the century for a child's garment. This, like the nightgowns worn by men, was probably a gown for everyday house wear, but it might mean the sashed wrap worn beneath the coat. Coats, frocks and nightgowns were the garments made for Harry and Kitty Furnese. Frocks were recorded only once when both were very small children, and these were made in quantity, "for making 8 frocks for the children 16s". Shortly afterwards, at a cost of £7 4s., "9 yards of silk for the children's coats" were bought. When Harry was still a baby he had "3 yards and a half of silk for a nightgown". In 1720 there were "two stript sattin nightgowns for the children".

The stiffened bodice disappeared for boys in the second half of the century, although they often, and girls sometimes, wore a frock with a cord lacing on the front, "a good fit, easy *juste* bodies with a satin cord to mark the bib shape in front" (*Mrs. Papendiek's Diary*, 1787).

Boys wore *leading strings* while they were in frocks and specially strong material was, apparently, made for them, showing that for boys of this age the strings were still functional:

> "Pray desire Cousen Peg to by me a pair of leading strings for Jak, there is stuf made on purpose that is very strong for he is so heavy. I dare not venture him with a comon ribin."
> 1715. John Verney was just under 4 years old. (Verney Letters of the Eighteenth Century.)

Leading strings gradually ceased to be used after the middle of the century, or at least, ceased to be a part of the dress. Another protective device for a child still uncertain on its feet was a *pudding*, a padded cap.

> "I wore a pudding when I was a little boy and all my mother's children wore puddings. This pudding consisted of a broad black

silk band which went round the middle of the head, joined to two pieces of ribband crossing on the top of the head and then tied under the chin; so that by this most excellent contrivance children's heads were often preserved uninjured when they fell."
(*Nollekens and His Times*, J. T. Smith, 1828; Nollekens was born in 1737.)

Indoors boys discarded their caps much earlier than girls, and their hair was worn short, with a fringe:

"Frederick begins to walk alone and has left off his cap."
(Letter of Lady Grantham, 1784, Beds. County Record Office, L/30/9/81.)

They wore caps under their outdoor hats, and they wore night caps after they had discarded day caps. George Brudenell's linen in 1718, when he was 5, comprised:

"8 shirts, 4 Holland nightcaps, 8 muslin cuffs and collars, 12 handkerchiefs" (shared with his sister Frances).
(*Brudenells of Deene*, J. Wake, 1953.)

Hats were rather large and elaborate. At the beginning of the century they reflected the general style of hair and head dresses by having the brim turned up to make a high front. In the middle of the century the hats were flatter, and often had a single cock. By the 1780s they were large in crown and brim, once again reflecting women's fashions. These and dress hats throughout the century were often trimmed with plumes. Beaver was the usual material for boys' hats:

"Frederick's blue beaver was dyed black. I got a quilted black hat for Georgy."

(*Mrs. Papendiek*, 1788.)

Frederick had worn a blue beaver as a baby, but as a little boy of between 1 and 2 he wore a black hat. Georgy was younger and his quilted hat was probably of silk. A year later both little boys had black beaver hats. With these out of doors they wore great-coats of garter blue.

Small boys sometimes wore an *apron*, and under their frock they might wear a pocket, as girls and women did, a flat linen bag, tied round the waist with tapes. Witness this story in the *Juvenile Magazine*, 1788, of a little boy who wanted to go to bed wearing his pocket. Charles was eating cherries when he was called to go to bed. He put some cherries in his pocket, wished his Mamma good night and quietly departed.

> "He had not, however, left the room many minutes before his Mamma heard him scream violently. . . . 'I want my pocket. Nanny will not let me go to bed with my pocket on.'
> 'What Charles,' said his Mamma laughing, 'Would you have your pocket on now you are going to sleep?'
> 'I want my pocket on!' cried Charles.
> 'Well,' said this Mamma, . . . 'I will for once indulge you in this whim; but remember I tell you, that you are very silly to desire anything so absurd, and will repent when it is too late.'
> Charles continued crying, 'I want my pocket on' . . . and Nanny fetched the pocket and . . . Charles went to bed with his pocket on."

The next morning the cherries were, of course, all squashed, hence the moral.

When they were 3 or 4 (earlier than in the seventeenth century), boys were breeched, but some were kept in petticoats longer. If the identifications in Zoffany's painting of the family of Lord Willoughby de Broke are correct, boys of 6 and 7 were wearing long white frocks and blue sashes in 1770. Mrs. Papendiek, recalling many years later the breeching of her own son, Frederick at the age of 4, in 1790, said:

> "Boys being in breeches was a convenience in comparison to their wearing frocks or jean or nankeen tunics, which the higher ranks usually kept till their boys were six or seven."

Charles, the son of Lord Romney, was, however, breeched at the age of 3 in 1747:

> "Charles makes a much better figure in breeches than I could have imagined, for he is considerably shorter than our boy (who was about the same age) and my Lord scolds me vastly for keeping him in petticoats."
>
> (*Admiral's Wife.*)

PLATE 13

Little boy in collarless coat with deep round cuffs and scalloped pocket flaps; roll-up stockings and shoes with turnover
scalloped tongues. He wears a long cravat and a sword. 1705–8.

*"Garton Orme (1696–1758) at the spinet". Attributed to Thomas Hill
(1661–1724). Reproduced by kind permission of the Trustees of Holburne
Museum, Bath*

PLATE 14

Charles, aged 3 years, and Henry, aged 1 year, sons of Lord Cornwallis.
Charles is breeched, Henry still in petticoats. 1742.

From the Collection at Audley End
Reproduced by kind permission of the Hon. Robin H. C. Neville

Her son, Edward, was breeched later in the same year, when he was 4.

Until the 1780s, a boy, once he was breeched was dressed in a small replica of his father's, coat, waistcoat and breeches. The coat followed the lines of men's coats, fitted to the waist where it flared into a skirt to the knees; the skirt, in the 1730s and 1740s, was stiffened and pleated at the side vents; there was also a vent at the centre back. The sleeves rather loose early in the century, but becoming closer in fit, sometimes ended in a turn-back cuff or, more usually, were slit so that they could be turned back and the slit closed by buttoning. There were pockets with flaps, just below waist level. The coat buttoned down the front from neck to hem until about 1735 and then to the waist level: occasionally an edge to edge fastening under frogs was used in the early part of the century. Later, in the 1770s, boys' coats, like those of men, fastened at the top only, with the buttons now ornamental. After 1750, the width of the skirt lessened, the side vents moved towards the back and the fronts curved away from the opening. By the 1780s the fronts were beginning to be cut away, square, at the waist level and the skirt

Twin boys wearing wigs; black neck ribbons;
coat sleeves with slit cuff, closed. *c.* 1760.
(Christchurch Mansion, Ipswich.)

C.C.E.–H

remained only as a tail at the back. A suit in fawn corduroy, in Salford Museum, has curved fronts, taken round to a short, narrow tail, and is an interesting example of an everyday suit showing the transition between the two styles. There was no collar to the "coats" until the 1760s when a small, standing collar appeared, but the *frock*, an undress coat, with a small, turn-down collar was also worn from the 1730s. This followed the same lines as the dress coat, but was generally looser and simpler in cut and fabric: it was nearly always made in woollen cloth. By the 1780s this form sometimes had lapels, which grew wider in the 1790s.

The waistcoat also resembled the adult waistcoat, reaching almost to the knees, but always a little shorter than the coat, at the beginning of the century. Its skirt shortened until, in the 1770s, it was at about hip level, with a V-shaped cut at the lowest button. In the first half of the century it was often sleeved; the sleeves were usually without cuffs and like the coat had a slit at the wrist which could be buttoned or left open. It had pockets like those of the coat but smaller, and straight-welted pockets from about 1780. By this time the waistcoat had become still shorter with the base square-cut at the waist. Double-breasted waistcoats with small lapels and standing collar had also appeared. Boys playing cricket and other games generally seem to have worn waistcoat and breeches only.

Boy in dark blue "frock", scarlet waistcoat, ruffled shirt. He holds a "round hat" and a cricket bat. Natural hair. *c.* 1775. (Master Dillon by Sir Joshua Reynolds.)

Knee breeches were worn by all boys until the 1780s, and by older boys until the last years of the century. These were buckled below the knee where they ended in a band and a short slit in the outer seam, which fastened with four or five buttons. Breeches were made on a waistband which laced or buckled at the back to tighten them round the waist, for they were worn without support until the late 1780s, when braces appeared; Helyar Wyndham, born in 1778, had a pair, called *Gallowses* brought for him in 1794. (Wyndham MSS., Devizes.) In the early years of the century breeches were closed down the centre front with buttons, without a fly, but by 1730 a turn-down flap or *fall* covering the opening was more usual. A "whole fall" was a large flap extending the full width of the front, fastened to the waistband at the sides and in the centre; a "half fall" covered the centre section only. There were pockets in the side seams and pockets with a horizontal opening, and sometimes with flaps, at the waist-band in front.

Dress suits which might be made in silk, plain, figured or velvet, were often made with coat, waistcoat and breeches all matching, but the waistcoat might be in a contrasting silk. Materials were often richly figured, or plain materials were trimmed with silver lace or embroidered. The everyday dress of boys who on occasion wore

Frock with square cut-away and wide lapels; hair still worn over the ears. 1795. (John Adam by H. Edridge.)

these elegant garments and the dress of unfashionable children might also be a suit of matching garments, but plainer, in one of the stronger silks, in woollen fabric, in corduroy or stout cotton or linen. These too might have a contrasting, not a matching, waistcoat, or they might be composed of garments, each of a different colour and fabric. A missing boy of 1748 was wearing:

> "a dark blue-grey Broad Cloth coat lin'd with the same colour, with brass moulded buttons, the brass of one button on his sleeve and hip are dropped off from the moulds. His waitcoat is camblet, with some flat white metal and silk buttons: his breeches are blue-grey Broad cloth and blue-grey mohair buttons; the right knee of his breeches is ripped up on the inside from the knee-garter."
>
> (*Daily Advertiser*, 26th October.)

Leather breeches were often worn. George Brudenell of Deene was given buckskin breeches at the age of 10, and leather breeches seem to have been worn by boys of all classes. A missing apprentice in York in 1777, who was "near 17 years old" had on when he went away:

Matching frock and breeches with contrasting, gold-laced waistcoat: hair brushed forward and long at back, *c.* 1770. John, Earl of Mexborough, b. 1761, by B. Wilson, York City Art Gallery.)

"a brown jacket and yellow waistcoat with brass buttons leather breeches a pair of brown broad-ribbed stockings and a gold button and loop to his hat."

(*York Chronicle,* 14th March.)

Black silk breeches were also very generally worn. Black was worn for mourning, but seems also to have had a much more general use. A gay little girl of 11 wrote to her brother in 1759 describing how she had dressed herself up in his clothes:

"You cant think how many kisses I have had on your account this Xmas. Dressed in your velvet breeches, blak coat, etc. etc. I make so smart a lad. . . ." Signed "Jacky Chubb".
(*A Forbear and his Hobby,* M. Chubb, *The Countryman,* winter 1963–4.)

Knitted waistcoats were worn at the end of the century.

"5 lads waistcoats made of Jersey with sleeves to them and 4 of green frizze with sleeves."

(*Ipswich Journal,* 1786.)

These were probably, with their sleeves, unfashionable waistcoats. Coat and breeches were lined, also the waistcoat fronts; the backs were of wool, linen or cotton.

Once a boy was breeched he was a very complete small man:

"Being four years and a half old and dressed in my best suit, a cocked hat and walking stick my sister took me by the hand to Gilbert Bridge's for the evening milk, which in future was to be my errand. One of his buxom daughters in a gay mood snatched off my hat. . . . I gave her a blow with my stick: she returned the hat."

1727. (*Life of Wm. Hutton* by himself.)

The *stick* was carried in place of the sword, which was still part of the dress of finer young gentlemen, especially when they were in full dress. A *cocked hat* had either a single cock, i.e. a turn-up of the brim, or three, making the three-cornered hat which was the most popular form of the eighteenth century. This was worn by boys until the 1770s; it was often trimmed with gold or silver braid:

"The young gentlemen of Mr. Fountayne's boarding school . . . walked two and two, some in pea-green, others in sky-blue and several in the brightest scarlet; many of them wore gold-laced hats, while the flowing locks of others at that time allowed to remain uncut at schools, fell over their shoulders."

1774. (*A Book for a Rainy Day*, J. T. Smith, 1845.)

In *The Young Gentleman's Polite Tutor* (1770), there are instructions about the wearing of hats, particularly when dancing:

"If the hat is too large in the crown or too little, the first will be difficult to keep in its proper place and the latter will be equally as bad to take off. The hat should always be cocked unless the weather be bad to prevent it. Nothing makes a Man appear more clownish than a slouched hat, and particularly in a Dancing School or in dancing a Minuet. To have the brim of your hat large and the crown high is awkward; it is always foppish to have your hat too little, that is not to appear larger than a Scotch bonnet or a Jockey's cap (this seems to be the present frothy fashion)."

The *slouched hat* was the *round hat,* with rather large round, flat-topped crown and wide brim which was just coming into use and had by the end of the century replaced the cocked hat in all but full dress wear, for older boys. A black velvet *jockey cap* was often worn by boys, particularly, of course, as a riding hat.

After they had left off their frocks in the early years of the century boys wore their *hair* rather long, parted in the centre and falling on to the shoulders, often curling at the ends. From the 1740s it was generally worn shorter over the ears, but still long at the back. At schools there were regulations about keeping the hair short. Boys at Lawidam School were instructed, in 1751, not "to wear long curled frizzed or powdered or ruffin-like hair, or to cut it in such a manner that the beauty of their forehead might be seen and that the hair should not grow longer than above one inch below the tips of their ears" (Journal of Walter Gale, Sussex Arch. Colln. IX, 1857). Boys sometimes wore wigs. A wig was bought for Harry Furnese when he was about 10 years old, in 1725:

"Periwig for Harry 3. 0. 0. Black velvet cap for Harry 9. 0." (Op. cit.)

The black velvet cap was probably a "jockey" cap. Lady Sarah Osborne wrote of George Osborne, in 1746, when he was at most 5 years old:

> "If you see him soon you will be frighted, for he is not the same child, and monstrously disguised by a wig he has got on today. His hair is cut quite close and as soon as his head can be shaved, it must be so and his eyebrows too."
> (*Political and Social Letters of a Lady of the Eighteenth Century, 1721–71.*)

The Scottish boy who was being dressed in a sensible suit of woollen fabric in 1739 also had a wig ordered for him:

> ". . . clothes for my little boy Sandie, so I entreat you, go with him to any shop where you can get it most reasonable, and be so kind as to see him cut off as much good strong drugget as will make the child a coat, waistcoat and breeches, with lining and all other furniture conform. I hope his periwig is now ready, that you bespoke, and a little hat for him."
> (Letter from Lord Lovat, quoted in *Old Inverness*, Celtic Magazine, X.)

During the 1760s the hair was brushed forward in a fringe for older boys as well as younger ones and hair long to the shoulders was again worn, even by older boys. Flowing locks were worn by the boys of Mr. Fountayne's school in the 1770s, and by a boy of 15 in 1781:

> "I was a few days after our arrival (in Brunswick) at the opera, with my hair about my ears and my shirt collar open, like an English boy when Mr. Six was told the Duchess wished to see me in her box. I was of course presented to her Royal Highness Princess Augusta, [sister of George III] who immediately in a torrent of English, expressed delight in seeing what she had been accustomed to see in her own country, and insisted that I should come to Court as I was, in the teeth of etiquette; and so it was, excepting that I rigged myself out with a dress coat and ruffles and a sword instead of wearing common English clothes."
> (*Early Married Life of Maria Josepha, Lady Stanley*, ed. J. H. Adeane, 1899.)

This fashion continued until the 1790s, when young men themselves appeared wigless, and with close-cropped hair.

At the beginning of the century boys wore a *cravat* of lawn or muslin folded round the neck and tied once in front, with long ends, like that worn by men. By the 1740s, older boys, keeping to the fashion of their fathers, wore a cravat which was a plain folded band fastening at the back and revealing the frill of the shirt opening between it and the top of the waistcoat. Younger boys had a fashion of their own, a frilled shirt collar, usually tied up high to the neck with a narrow black ribbon, or sometimes a plain shirt band worn as a turn-down collar. During the 1770s the shirt was worn open with the frilled collar spread over the coat, the sight that so delighted the Princess Augusta. The shirt was usually made of linen, the frills of muslin.

Sometimes a flannel underwaistcoat was worn. Helyar Wyndham had two flannel waistcoats in 1794. He also had cotton *drawers*.

At the beginning of the century the stockings were sometimes drawn up over the breeches and rolled there, but this fashion disappeared in the 1740s and breeches were then buckled over the stockings. *Stockings* were in silk, cotton, thread (linen) or wool, according to the season, rank and occasion. In the Wyndham records twelve pairs of boys' worsted hose, costing £1. 1s. 11d. were bought in January 1787 for four boys, then between the ages of 9 and 14: in July twelve pairs of cotton ones were bought and twelve pairs of thread: and in the following January another fourteen pairs of worsted hose. They were generally white, but might be brown or grey for everyday wear:

> "3 pair Youths Grey Knitt hose."
>
> 1740. (Essex Record Office, D/D. R.C., F.23.)

For fashionable wear the stockings were of silk or cotton.

> "In the next place your stockings should be either silk or cotton. Take great care to have your stockings fit well and particularly in the feet . . . they sould be tied smooth and fast but not too tight. . . . Never be without clean white gloves in point of decency."
>
> (*The Young Gentleman's . . . Polite Tutor*, 1770.)

Shoes followed the styles of men until the end of the century. The uppers covered the foot ending in high square tongues over which straps from the heel leather buckled. Until the 1720s the toes were square and blocked and the heels also square and fairly high, but from this time the toes were rounded and the uppers and tongues were cut lower and the heels also lowered. The buckles tended to grow bigger, as the uppers grew lower and were particularly large in the 1770s, before they began to be replaced by shoe-strings. Buckles might be elaborate and expensive or very plain and simple, but until the last twenty years of the century they were generally worn. The buckles in the shoes of a missing apprentice were given as a means of recognition, in 1753,

> "he is a stout lad about five feet four inches high, had on when he went away a brown coat with white checkered buttons* on it, a blue waistcoat, black breeches, white thread stockings, a brown clipp'd wig, and had in his shoes a pair of yellow, cross barr'd Buckles".
>
> (*Ipswich Journal.*)

Boots were worn only for riding; these were knee-length, pulled on by loops each side. Pumps were worn for dancing: these had thin soft soles and no heels:

> "Your pumps must be thin soft and yielding Leather with no Heels the quarters neither short nor long but made in such manner so as when buckled may be close and easy to the foot. Every gentleman or lady should have their buckles bent to fit their feet. The tongues of the buckles ought to be very good as that will keep the pumps in their proper place, and should they be not good either too long or too short the first will make the ladies afraid to come nigh you (as their aprons too often experience the ill effects thereof) and the latter will prevent your dancing or even walking with pleasure."
>
> (*The Young Gentleman's . . . Polite Tutor*, 1770.)

The Young Gentleman's . . . Polite Tutor also had something to say about the way to wear clothes,

> "You are to avoid dressing yourself as you walk along the street or

---

* Buttons, like buckles, could also be costly and decorative or very plain and were made in a wide range of materials.

when you are in a room. . . . I will give you an example by showing you that inimitable Fop Mr. Gaudy! Now you see him, there
he is . . . observe him rubbing his hands. . . . These kind of people
be in Lamb-skin gloves and go to great expense in buying Waters
to wash their Hands in to make them look fair. But observe him
pulling down his Shirt Sleeves, now placing his Ruffles, there now
his Neckcloth, there now placing his Hat . . . now his shirt is not
right, now he is placing his neckcloth, now his finger is in his hair
. . . now his coat sleeves are pulled down, they are not low enough
and if you were to follow him all day he would not be rightly
dressed."

In the 1780s there was a change in the dress of younger boys who
now appeared in a distinctive style, which made a new period of
transition between the frock and sash of babyhood and the breeches
which had turned little boys all at once into men. With its introduction the full pattern of eighteenth-century dress was broken. A
new garment, *trousers,* was adopted by boys, and this was ultimately accepted for men's dress. Thus the form that had persisted
for over a century, coat, waistcoat and breeches changed to the
nineteenth-century form of coat, waistcoat and trousers.

Trousers were not a completely new garment. They had been
worn in Ireland and Scotland and by sailors and sometimes by
countrymen. But they had never yet been a garment in general
fashion in England, until they first appeared amongst small boys in
the 1780s:

> "Tommy (born December 1781) has a new jacket and trousers."
> (Letter of Lady Grantham, August 1785, Beds. County Record
> Office, L/30/9/81.)

Trousers as they now appeared were of two kinds, one with
rather wide leg, the other the tight-fitting *pantaloon.* The former
was a lengthening and narrowing of the open-legged breeches which
had been worn by boys in the seventeenth century, and which in
unfashionable wear had probably never completely disappeared.
The boys at the Foundling Hospital in 1747 were dressed in:

> "only one garment which is made jacket fashion of Yorkshire
> serge, with a slip of red cloth across the shoulder; their shirts lapping

over their collar resembling a cape. Their breeches hang loose a great way down their legs; instead of buttons is a slip of red cloth furbelowed."

(*The Gentleman's Magazine*, June 1747.)

Pantaloons began in a lengthening of breeches below the knee, as worn with riding boots, and ultimately reached the ankle. Both the tighter and the looser forms appear during the 1780s at all lengths between the knee and the ankle, but by the end of the century both were usually longer, ending at the ankle or just above it. There was often a short slit at the ankle.

When the coat (which was often cut away square at the front by the 1770s) was worn with a waistcoat and over the breeches or pantaloons, its short, narrow tails might remain. But a new jacket form, without the tails and worn without a waistcoat was used by younger boys. They often appeared in this with a sash at the waist;

Girl's outdoor dress: boy with open, frilled shirt, trousers, coat with curved fronts and narrow tail. *c.* 1785. (From a print "Christmas Holiday" by J. R. Smith.)

then, as the jacket grew shorter, in accordance with the rising waistline of all dress of the time, the trousers were buttoned on to and over the jacket. Mrs. Papendiek's son Frederick wore a suit of this kind when he was breeched at the age of 4 in 1790.

> "On this day our dear Frederick was breeched, and a total change of dress it was then for a boy. The shirt was made like a man's except that the collar was large and frilled and turned over the jacket instead of being buttoned up. The jacket and trousers were of cloth, the latter being buttoned over the jacket and the trousers only to the ankle bone. Boots for children being then unknown they had gaiters which went over the end of the trousers, and these with strong shoes equipped them very properly for walking. The great coat of the preceding year came in again, but he had a new hat and cane. . . . Underwaistcoats and drawers were not then worn, so I had the linings of the trousers made separate which ensured proper cleanliness."
>
> (Op. cit.)

This became known as a *skeleton suit* and was to be the distinctive dress of boys between the ages of 3 and 7 for the next forty years.

. . .

Until the 1760s little girls from the time they were about 2 years old, were dressed in a style which appeared very like that worn by their mothers.

The dress of their mothers for most of this period was a robe and petticoat, the robe open down the front, its bodice, shaped by the stays beneath, fastened over a stomacher in front, its skirt falling open to reveal the petticoat. This style was worn by older girls only. The dress of younger girls also had the tight-fitting, cone-shaped bodice with low neck and elbow-length sleeves, and a long, full skirt to the ground, but their bodice fastened at the back and the skirt was separate. The neck line tended to form a rounded décolletage rather than the squared one of women's dress; and the sleeves were a little shorter, ending well above the elbow, though a little longer by the middle of the century. The sleeves of the smock or shift, either gathered into a plain band or a frilled one, were visible below.

The short sleeve had a cuff, which followed the fashionable shaping; wide and softly pleated, often caught up with a button or ribbon till the 1740s; then a plain, turn-back cuff was worn and also a plain sleeve, over which a frilled muslin cuff was worn in addition to the falling sleeve frill beneath (Pl. 15). All these styles were worn in the 1740s, but the wide pleated cuff had disappeared by the 1750s. There was a tucker or frill of muslin or lace at the neck. The dress was completed by a bib and apron, the bib following the pointed shape of the bodice (Pl. 15). A child's dress, a bodice and skirt of white silk, brocaded in silver, with its muslin bib and cuffs still in place on the bodice, is preserved in King's Lynn Museum. By family tradition this was worn by a *boy* in 1751. For full dress apron and bib were elaborately edged with lace, and were of fine linen, muslin or silk: "Lace, ribans, silk for short aprons" were bought for Mally Blundell (quoted in *Blundell's Diary and Letter Book* 1952) when she was 13, in 1717. The bib and apron were also for everyday wear. Christian Williamson, who was not quite 7 years old, had a black silk bib and apron to wear every day, in 1759:

> "I have bought her a black bib and apron to wear every day, which is very genteel and will keep her frocks and slips clean."
> (Williamson Letters, Beds. Hist. Rec. Soc., 1954.)

Another style of dress was a wrapping gown, with a wrap-over fastening in front. A girl of 12 had "6 yards of printed calico for a wrapper gown, 17s." in 1709, and, in the following year, "for the materials of durance scarlet for a wrapping gown and the making", her father gave £2. 3s. 9d. Although this woollen fabric was more expensive than the printed calico, both of these gowns suggest dress for everyday wear. In the same year this girl's "new gown, petty-cotes, etc., cost £15. 2s., so presumably these were silk; in the previous year she had "mantle, petticoate, silk, scarlet stockings, bought in London" which cost £16. 16s. (Diary of Timothy Burrell, Sussex Arch. Colln. III, 1850.)

In the 1770s and early 1780s older girls wore the polonaise, a robe with the skirt caught up in puffs by cords inside and drawn back to show more of the petticoat. Sylas Neville saw, at a concert in

London, "a lovely girl about fourteen in a purple polonese and pink sash" in 1783 (Diary of Sylas Neville, 1767–88, 1950). By this time too older girls were also wearing the long, tight-fitting sleeves, which were fashionable during the 1780s and 1790s.

The materials of the dresses worn by girls were often rich and elaborate, damasked figured and brocaded silks, similar to those of women's dresses (Pl. 16) until well into the second half of the century. The Furnese family was a wealthy one, but Kitty Furnese was only about 8 years old when "red and white silk for a coat for Kitty" cost £7, in 1722. In the following year she had 10½ yards of green and white lustring for a coat, which was less expensive, £4. 9s., and an extra piece of red and white silk "to make a pair of sleeves to Kitty's coat". These may have been the hanging sleeves and were perhaps a replacement of original ones. Coat in this entry seems to mean a full-length garment, and in 1726 she had 10 yards of silk "for the skirt of a coat", a good deal of material for the skirt of a girl of 12, even if the silk was the usual 18–20 inch width. Printed linens and cottons were in general use for everyday wear in the middle of the century. Christian Williamson's uncle was buying material for her gowns in London, in 1757:

> "As to the 3 yards and a half for little Miss . . . there is no tolerable linen with a dark ground at that price, 4s or 4s 6d the lowest. However none of the young ladies in London can bear to wear a dark ground—they like to have a white linen with a pink pattern."
>
> (Op. cit.)

By now a gown seems to be the morning gown and a frock the garment of greater consequence,

> "The purple and white cotton . . . I would not cut it out in a gown, as I thought it too pretty for that use, and fancy you (? can make a) little frock of it!"
>
> (Ibid.)

The bodice of the dress was worn over a boned *pair of stays* to give the correct, fashionable shape, and even with the looser gowns stays were worn, and worn from a very early age. Mr. Blundell spent

£1. 10s. 9½d. on "material and whalebone for stays and stuff for a coat" for his daughter Mally when she cannot have been older than 3. (Op. cit.) Timothy Burrell paid £2. 4s. "To Venlowe for stayes" for his 13-year-old daughter in 1709 (op. cit.) and there is an entry, "For covering Kitty's stays with Norwich crape, and for making the skirt and petticoat" in the Furnese accounts in 1727. In the *Ipswich Journal* in 1766 a staymaker advertises as a "child's coat, slip and robe-maker, pack-thread stays as well as others". Christian Williamson had a *slip* made by a staymaker in 1759:

> "I thought proper to ask your staymakers, Mr. Rhodes," writes her aunt, "who would not make the slip under 10s 6d, so then, as I knew that was very unreasonable, I was determined to ask my own, who is to have 7s.; but I saw him measure it, and there must be a yard of damask more for hanging sleeves and 1½ yards of persian more; but the washing slip seems to be so awkward a pattern, and as he never saw her, that he greatly wishes to have the stays, as it is a great pity to spoil so handsome a thing. Therefore should think you might send them. . . . As to having hanging sleeves to the linen slips, 'tis of no consequence for such little folk, for they only dirty and look trolloping."
>
> (Op. cit.)

Christian was not quite 7 at this time. The damask was 8s. 6d. a yard, and the persian, a thin silk often used for linings, 2s. for the 1½ yards needed. From this account a *slip* seems to be the unboned bodice of the gown, which was to be made to fit the stays exactly. In *The Young Gentleman's and Lady's Polite Tutor* (1770), the importance of this is again emphasised:

> "I would recommend to those who would have their children appear decent and genteel to take care that their children's slips fit very exactly on the shoulders for it is of infinite service to those who are inclinable to grow high-shouldered it helps to keep their shoulders down and in their proper place."

Stays were of importance in giving the fashionable carriage, and for this another 9-year-old girl, had, in 1780 "girts to be fastened on the top of the stays and crossed over the shoulder blades and fastened before which will not appear being under the slip, to keep her back flat for a year or so".

(Mrs. Delany, *Autobiography and Correspondence*, 1861-2.)

Poorer girls wore leather bodices or stays: Elizabeth Linsell, who was apprenticed to a tailor in 1731 was given "a pair of leather boddice 2s 6d" (E. Simcoe, *Short History . . . Thaxted*, 1934). The girls of the Charity Hospital in Bedford were also given leather bodices in 1773, and the trustees spent £6. 8s. for "6 pairs of children's stays" in 1783. In *Instructions for Cutting Out Apparel for the Poor* (1789), stays are listed and the material for their making, half a yard and 1½ nails of duck, cane, lace and thread. The lace here is a stay lace for lacing them up, not the decorative fabric. But by the last decade of the century, younger girls wore only corded bodices and the stays proper were first worn at about the age of 10. Elizabeth Ham who was born in 1783, describes this process in growing-up:

"The first reformation in my appearance was effected by a stay-maker. I was stood on the window seat whilst a man measured me for the machine, which in consideration of my youth, was to be only what was called half-boned, that is instead of having the bones placed as close as they could lie, an interval, the breadth of one was left vacant between each. Notwithstanding, the first day of wearing them was very nearly purgatory, and I question if I was sufficiently aware of the advantage of a fine shape to reconcile me to the punishment."

1793. (*Elizabeth Ham by Herself*, 1783-1820, 1945.)

Although boys generally wore leading strings until they were breeched, for girls, leading strings remained as a symbolic ornament on their frocks, long after the need for them had passed. Christian Williamson had them on her best damask slip, but not on her every-day linen ones, because, as her aunt said (quoted above), "They only dirty and look trolloping", and emphasising their complete loss of purpose, "for 'tis of no consequence for such little folk". They became synonymous with girlhood:

PLATE 15

Two girls wearing bibs and aprons and frilled cuffs over their
short sleeves, with the frilled shift sleeves showing below;
both wear caps. The baby has a cap and undercap. The boy has
a frilled shirt-collar, a black neck ribbon, and a slit cuff to his
coat. 1742.

"The Graham Children". Hogarth
Reproduced by courtesy of the Trustees of the Tate Gallery, London

PLATE 16

Catherine (seated), aged 12, Anne, aged 9. Each wears a low-necked back-fastening bodice with a tucker. The sleeve has a frilled cuff above its edge, and the frilled sleeve of the shift shows below. 1742.

The daughters of Viscount Fauconberg. P. Mercier (signed and dated)
Reproduced by kind permission of Captain V. M. Wombwell
On loan to Temple Newsam House, Leeds

"Ev'n misses at whose age their mothers wore
The backstring and the bib assume the dress
Of womanhood"

(Cowper, *The Task*, IV.)

but were disappearing from dresses by the 1760s.

Hoop petticoats of cane or whalebone were fashionable between 1710 to 1780 to give the skirt of the dress its full fashionable shape; references to the wearing of them by young girls are scarce, but Kitty Furnese can hardly have been more than 3 years old when she

White silk dress, brocaded in colours (pattern omitted); separate skirt, fastens at back; back-lacing bodice has leading strings. Mid-eighteenth century. (Liverpool Museum. Drawn by S. Gregory.)

C.C.E.–I

had a hoop petticoat in 1716; she had another in 1720; the first cost
6s., the second 7s. They were certainly worn by girls who were just
becoming young women:

> "Miss P. came over. She is grown quite a young woman . . . her
> hair dressed without powder and a linnen gown with a small
> hoop."
>
> 1785. (Jerningham Letters, 1896.)

Hoops were at this time being replaced by *bustles*. Mrs. Papendiek's daughters wore small bustles under their concert dresses of
gauze.

Other *underwear* included the smock or shift. Timothy Burrell's
daughter had 4 ells of holland "for shifts", costing £2. 6s. in 1708,
when she was 12 (op. cit.). Frances Brudenell, when she was 6
or 7 years old, in 1718, had six shifts and two dimity night shifts.
There were under petticoats of flannel and linen or cotton, "white
dimotte for two under petticoats for Kitty" appear in the Furnese
accounts in 1723. The age of the daughter for whom Mrs. Western
was buying underwear in 1731 is unknown, but this included a
scarlet quilted petticoat (perhaps the visible one?) 14s. 5d., two flannel
and two dimothy petticoats, 12s. (Essex Record Office, D/DU/77/1.)

Dress with tucker, sleeves with ruffled
undersleeves and frilled cuffs; apron
embroidered at hem; ribbon and pompon of
flowers in her hair. 1762. (The Edgar
Family by A. Devis. Detail.)

There is no mention of drawers. Pockets were worn tied round the waist beneath the petticoat.

Included in the linen were the tuckers for the neck and sleeves and sleeve *ruffles*. Mr. Blundell bought for his 12- and 13-year-old daughters, "Linnen apparell for my children, viz. shifts, heads and ruffles." *Heads* refers to their linen caps, which were worn by night and by day. Frances Brudenell's linen included, as well as shifts and night shifts, "6 holland night caps, 4 quilted caps, 8 pair thread mittens, 2 white muslin hoods". The *tucker* was a frill of muslin or lace which edged the low neck of the dress. The sleeves were detachable sleeves of linen, gathered in a band, plain or edged with muslin or lace frills, worn over the shift sleeve, and appearing below the elbow-length sleeve of the dress. Sleeve ruffles might be falling ruffles added to these or to the smock sleeve, or the frilled cuff which girls wore over the sleeve itself.

Day caps of white linen and lace trimmed with ribbons were often worn, although at any time throughout the century a girl may appear without one in her portrait. Rather plain caps with "stays" meeting under the chin were worn in the 1720s and 1730s. From the 1730s to the 1750s flat caps with frills or with crown fitting closer to the head were the usual style; the frill was often pinched at the centre front as it was in women's caps. From the late 1740s to the early 1760s a flower or feather sometimes replaced the cap, for dress wear, or flowers and ribbons were added to the cap. According to *The Young Gentleman's and Lady's Polite Tutor*, in 1770:

> "For young ladies from three to fourteen years old a Feather, a Flower, Egret or Ribband or Pompon. These are proper for dancing in. Ladies above this age may do as they please."

A *pompon* was an ornament for the hair, made of feather, ribbon, lace, etc.,

> " 'How do you like my pompon Papa?' putting her hand to her head and showing me in the middle of her hair a complication of shreads, and rags of velvet, feathers and ribbands stuck with false stones of a thousand colours."
>
> (Lord Chesterfield, *The World*, 1753.)

Feather worn as head ornament, *c.* 1745.
(Elizabeth Hatch by Hogarth.)

But the cap was re-appearing in a large, more elaborate form from
the late 1760s. It now had a ruched border and during the 1770s this
with a high crown made an arched frame for the face. In the 1780s the
crown of the cap became more balloon-like—this decade was much
influenced by the new invention of the balloon—and soft muslin
frills replaced the ruche. It was now usually trimmed with a broad
ribbon to match the sash on the frock:

> "I took the little girls who also appeared with me in their new pink
> sashes and new caps with ribbon to match."
>
> (Mrs. Papendiek, *Diary*, 1789.)

Charlotte Papendiek, who was born in 1783 was painted by
Hoppner in 1788 when she was about 5 wearing a white dress with
a blue sash and one of these large white caps with blue ribbon. For
evening, girls sometimes wore hats—Sylas Neville noticed at a concert, in 1783:

PLATE 17

The boy's breeches are buckled above the knee, a fashion of the 1750s and he wears a neck ribbon. The little girl, in tight bodice and plain skirt, wears a round-eared cap fashionable from 1730s to 1760s. *c.* 1750.

Heneage Lloyd and his sister. T. Gainsborough
Reproduced by permission of the Syndics of the Fitzwilliam Museum,
Cambridge

PLATE 18

The two boys in the fashion of the day, in coats without collars, ruffled shirt sleeves emerging below the coat sleeves with round cuffs. They wear wigs.

Reproduced by Courtesy of the National Portrait Gallery
Portrait by Richard Wilson c. 1751 of Prince George (future George III)
with the Duke of York

Both girls and the boy wear dresses with
sashes and caps, the older girl wears a large
fashionable hat over her cap. *c.* 1787. (From a
water colour of the children of Mrs.
Papendiek.)

"a lovely girl about fourteen. . . . Her fine black hair hanging in
artless ringlets under a little striped hat with white ribbons, put very
far back almost perpendicular to the head."

(*Diary*, 1767–88, 1950.)

Princess Augusta Sophia wrote to Mary Hamilton in about 1780:

"we now do our Hair in a new sort of fashion and we have hats all
day and no caps".

(*Letters and Diaries of Mary Hamilton*, 1756–1816, 1925.)

Caps were becoming less worn by the 1790s, although when worn
they were still high in the crown though smaller than those of the
1780s.

At the beginning of the century *the hair* was parted in the middle
and brushed back to show the ears, then worn fairly long at the

back. For all the first half of the century the brow and ears were visible. Sometimes in the 1740s and 1750s the hair appears to have been worn quite short especially by young girls. In the late 1760s and during the 1770s older girls had the hair raised from the forehead, reflecting the fashionable high hairdressing, and, if they were royal princesses, this happened to them while they were still young:

> "One should not imagine that girls of 10, 8 and 7 in Polonaises with their hair dressed upon high cushions with stiff large curls, powdered, pomatumed, small dress caps and diamond ornaments . . . could look well . . . but in fact they did."
>
> 1777. (Ibid.)

Powder was not usually worn on the hair by girls as young as this, but it was worn by girls just becoming young women. By the 1760s younger girls were beginning to wear a fringe. Mrs. Delany wrote about her great niece, aged 9:

> "I have tried her hair up, but her forehead is now too bald, tho' it will not appear so another year with a little management of shaving the young hair." (1780.)

Serena Holroyd wrote to her 15-year-old niece, Maria Josepha, about her hairdressing in 1786:

> "I am glad your hair is turned up, because I think you will look neater and better for it. . . . Might I advise . . . that you should learn to dress your hair a little yourself? I do not mean you should not have a hair dresser as often as you please; but I mean that you should know how to do it when occasion may require for you cannot imagine how inconvenient it is to be totally helpless sometimes."
>
> (*Girlhood of Maria Josepha Holroyd*, 1776–96, 1896.)

The fashionable style, now curled or frizzed out widely over the ears instead of being carried up high must have needed some skill to dress. By the 1780s girls up to the age of 16 were wearing their hair with a fringe or plain over the forehead and flowing loose over the shoulders, a style which lasted to the end of the century:

"A sweet girl of sixteen with a fine tall slim figure, a pretty face and her light hair hanging down her back, as was then the fashion. She wore a small evening hat of white chip, trimmed with white."

1789. (Mrs. Papendiek.)

Schoolgirls in Bath going to a ball in 1797 had their hair dressed for the occasion by

"Mr. Pope, the chief hairdresser in Bath and his two assistants . . . as the fashion then was . . . à la Brutus. If it had been called à la Porcupine or à la Hedgehog it would have been as well, for except the front row of curls round the face, which we were to put up ourselves as usual, the hairdressers screwed our hair up in innumerable curls all over our heads, and I am sure there never could have been seen at any time, so many funny figures sit down to dinner, or together anywhere . . . bristled all over with hard curl papers. . . . The next day, immediately after dinner, came the uncurling process."

1797–1800. (*Memoirs of Susan Sibbald, 1783–1812, 1926.*)

Gloves and mittens were both worn throughout the century. Frances Brudenell had eight pairs of thread mittens, that is probably those of knitted linen thread, in 1718. Two dozen white gloves, costing £1. 4s. were bought for the two Furnese children in 1720. Mrs. Papendiek's small daughters wore long skin gloves tied over the elbows "to preserve the arm in beauty for womanhood". They also wore elbow-length gloves with the fingers cut off so that they could always wear them. Mittens with the back of the hand shaped to a point and turned back to show the coloured silk lining, appear in portraits of the 1760s to 1780s. Poor girls wore gloves or mittens of knitted worsted.

Hand or machine-knitted *stockings* were worn, made of wool, silk, cotton or linen, kept up by garters, knitted or braided. Coloured stockings were very generally worn, particularly in the early and middle period of the century. Elizabeth Burrell had "a pair of fine scarlet stockings" which cost 3s. when she was 10, in 1706. A few months later her father bought her another pair, "I bought of a Scotchman a payr of pink scarlet stockings for my girl, a better pennyworth than Richardsons." Kitty Furnese had thread stockings with black clocks in 1724 and red silk stockings and three pairs of thread stockings in 1727. For the winter of 1788, Mrs. Papendiek provided worsted stockings for her three children, two girls and a boy between the ages of 1 and 5. By the end of the century white stockings were the usual wear.

Shoes were worn throughout the century: there seems to be no evidence for girls wearing boots. Their shoes had the fashionable front, straps which buckled or tied over a high tongue, and they

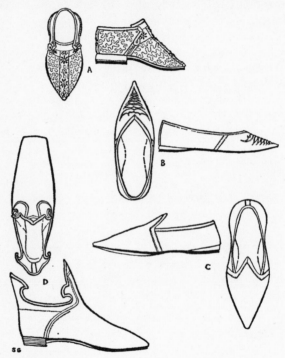

Shoes and boots
A embroidered linen, 1700–25.
B pink kid, 1790–1800.
C dark blue leather, bound cream silk, 1800–10.
D boy's half-boots, black leather, bound yellow ribbon, "collegians", 1820–40.
(Gallery of English Costume, Manchester. Drawn by S. Gregory.)

were made of leather, plain or trimmed, or of fabric. Unlike the
shoes of women, they had flat heels. They were black or coloured.
Kitty Furnese had a black leather pair in 1727, "Black Dansick
Leather shoes for Kitty yt was bought at Canterbury 5s 6d." Elizabeth
Burrell was 13 in 1709 when she had "2 pair of Turkey leather shoes,
one yellow, one red, laid with silver, 9s." Mrs. Papendiek's children
had chamois and sealskin shoes for walking and kid "for their best
and the house" in 1788. The tongue had by this time become lower
and buckles were disappearing as a means of fastening; the shoes tied
in front, or, by the end of the century had low fronts, trimmed with
ruched ribbon and a small bow. Susan Sibbald when she was at school
at Bath had a pair of black morocco shoes bound with "Coqlicot (a
bright scarlet the color of a blazing Comet geranium)". For walking
girls might wear *clogs* over their shoes. These were leather soled
overshoes, a sole with straps usually matching the shoe, which
fastened over the instep,

> "and in the dark of the alley I stopped pretending to mend the
> child's clog that was loose and took off her necklace".
> (*Moll Flanders*. D. Defoe, 1722.)

In the country *pattens* were worn. These were wooden soles,
raised on iron rings, fastened over the foot by leather straps. A girl
who was apprenticed in Braintree in 1735 was provided with shoes
and patterns (*Short History . . . Thaxted, E. Simco*, 1934). Both
clogs and pattens were worn by women as well as children.

Out of doors *cloaks*, short or full-length, with or without hoods,
of silk or wool, were worn for most of the century, although *overcoats*, which were occasionally mentioned earlier, came into more
general use in the 1780s. Elizabeth Burrell had a scarlet camlet cloak,
in 1710, when she was 14, a handsome one, which cost £3. 9s.
Scarlet cloaks were the characteristic wear of English countrywomen
throughout the century. The silk cloaks were very often black. Mrs.
Papendiek's children wore double-breasted great-coats in 1789, the
girls dark blue coats of ladies' cloth, with two rows of very small
yellow-knobbed buttons down the front, the boys finest Bath coating of the same blue. Short shoulder capes called *tippets* were also

worn, apparently sometimes in fur, for winter, at least by one girl, Elizabeth Tufnell; when she was nearly 17 in 1703, her father bought her a "sables tippet" for which he gave £11. 5s. Tippets were worn until the end of the century, but in the 1790s, a short, long-sleeved jacket, the spencer, was an alternative:

> "being Summer at 4 o'clock bonnets, spencers, or tippets, and walking shoes on, and attended by the 3 Teachers we . . . took a walk into the country".
>
> (Memoirs of Susan Sibbald.)

The "whisk" that was bought for Christian Williamson in 1759 was probably a tippet,

> "I have also got her a bonnet and whisk for her when she goes out. . . . I hope the whisk will fit her too."
>
> (Op. cit.)

Jackets were worn for riding; these are very like boys' coats but usually have the front skirts cut separately and seamed.

Outdoor hats and bonnets were generally, though not invariably, worn over a cap until the 1780s. Hoods were worn too, particularly at the beginning of the century. Mr. Blundell bought "lace, ribans,

Girl's riding jacket, fawn wool, with waistcoat fronts, matching silk; metal buttons. Mid-eighteenth century. (Gallery of English Costume, Manchester. Drawn by S. Gregory.)

silk for aprons and huds" for his daughters in 1717. The hoods, like
the cloaks were often of black silk. In the 1730s small hats with
conical crowns—witches' hats—were popular and this style was worn
by girls of the Foundling Hospital in 1747. During the middle years
of the century, from the 1740s to 1760s, a flat-crowned hat with a
fairly wide brim, in straw, chip, silk or beaver, was worn. Sometimes
the wide brim was worn turned up at one side, and it was often worn
with a ribbon over the crown, tied under the chin, thus drawing the
brim downwards into a bonnet shape. Christian Williamson's aunt,
writing about the new bonnet she had bought for her niece, said:

> "Don't be frightened at its bigness, for 'tis all the fashion, and is a
> very pretty one, and what every creature now wears, only they are
> mostly white; but thought that would dirty too fast." (1759.)

At a charity school in Middlesex, an annuity was given in 1764
to buy hats for the girls, hats very exactly specified:

> "for buying yearly straw hats, green and white, such as the girls
> now have and were made at Dunstable, a pattern of which is pre-
> served; the brims not to exceed 5½"; and not to be lined; but to be
> tied on with a green silk riband such as is now sold for 6d yard".
> (Beds. County Record Office, W3271.)

Single-breasted great coat with large,
fashionable hat. 1786. (From a
print "Winter".)

In the 1770s the crown began to grow higher and balloon hats, with full, soft crowns and sloping brims were popular, often looking far too big for the small girls who wore them. Gainsborough's painting of Miss Haverfield, in the Wallace Collection, shows one of these hats, elaborately trimmed, worn over a cap. She is also wearing a black silk cloak. Copley's painting of the three younger daughters of George III in 1785 shows one bareheaded, one with a large hat far back on the head, and the baby a large plumed hat over a cap. Mrs. Papendiek's daughters wore lined straw bonnets and these they seemed to wear for winter as well as summer, "Their straw bonnets, cleaned, now again looked almost new, and were lined and trimmed with lustring (now termed gros de Naples)—Mrs. Papendiek was probably writing in the 1830s—of the same colour." Wide brimmed straw hats worn with a ribbon over the crown were still popular, but the crown was higher than it had been in the middle of the century. During the 1790s hats with a high crown and narrow brim appeared. In the accounts of the Wyndham family, of Devizes, there is an entry for "A girl's deep crown straw hat 4s 6d with pink persian and ribbon and wire for making." This was for

Girls of 9 and 14 in tall-crowned hats, 1791 (from *The Blind Child* by Mrs. Pinchard)

PLATE 19

Boy aged 10, behind the stumps, boy with bat aged 14. Their coats and hats are discarded showing waistcoats with flapped pockets. The hair is worn short. 1733.

"Cricket Scene at Harrow School Playing Fields." (Detail). *H. Walton. Reproduced by kind permission of Mrs Claude Partridge*

PLATE 20

The cricketers without coats, in kneebreeches or pantaloons. Boys with the kite in short coats and open shirts with wide frilled collars. 1800.

Mezzotint "The Soldier's Widow: or School Boys' Collection" by Robert Dunkarton after William Redmore Bigg Reproduced by permission of the Syndics of the Fitzwilliam Museum, Cambridge

Miss Wyndham, who was married in 1797. In 1788 two other hats had been bought for her, "A young lady's cinnamon colour riding hat and stamp 16s, ribbon brocade band 8s." and "a black beaver hat and stamp 11s 6d." The stamp was necessary because of the hat tax imposed at this time.

Masks to protect the complexion were still, at the beginning of the century, occasionally worn by older girls, "a black mask 2s 6d" appears in the accounts for Elizabeth Tufnell in 1702 (*Samuel Tufnell of Langleys, 1682–1758,* F. W. Steer, 1960), when she was 16. *Fans* were part of a girl's full dress all through the century. Kitty Furnese had a fan costing 3s. in 1716, and later a fan paper, 2s. In 1720 she had a rather more expensive fan and fan paper 10s.; and in the next year a black and white fan at 5s. Fan papers were probably the painted leaves fashionable at the time; she might possibly have been painting her own. At the end of the century girls, like women, carried their fans to church. Susan Sibbald and the girls of Miss Lee's school at Bath:

> "set out for Church . . . and every girl had to carry a prayer book, and a fan which each had to hold before her face when praying. The sticks were like a Venetian blind, which you could look through without being seen yourself."

These were probably the fans which had separate sticks, not a single leaf.

Some *jewellery* was worn, mainly simple necklaces and earrings. Kitty Furnese had her ears bored for earrings in 1725:

> "For a little pair of gold Earrings for Kitty and Boaring her ears, 11s 6d."

Moll Flanders stole a little necklace of gold beads which the child in clogs was wearing, as she stooped down to attend to the loose clog. (*Moll Flanders,* D. Defoe, 1722.)

Dress for girls began to show an increasing difference from women's from the 1760s, although this was at first apparent only in the dress of younger girls. In the 1750s a girl of 4 wore a miniature of fashionable dress, but in the 1760s girls were continuing to wear for a little longer the low-necked frocks of muslin or linen with a sash at the waist which they had worn as babies, and which were now being worn by boys until they were breeched. The age for wearing this style rose, until by the 1780s girls in their teens were wearing it. A mother wrote to her 15-year-old daughter, who was being educated in a French convent, in 1786, "The white dresses are certainly the prettiest at your age and are worn entirely here by young people, with sashes" (*Jerningham Letters*, 1896). The Papendiek children had new gauze frocks in 1787 "with easy *juste* bodice with a satin cord to mark the bib shape in front, and so arranged as not to cut the stuff for letting out or fashioning next Spring. Under the frocks they wore gauze handkerchiefs, laid quite across in front, small bustles and a few well-placed bows." Frocks were still usually open down the back for children:

> "My sister being now in her fifteenth year and very much grown, we planned a trifling change in dress for her. Pretty printed cambric muslins made round were to be her gowns instead of frocks open behind in the skirts."
>
> (Mrs. Papendiek.)

But Mrs. Papendiek's own daughters had dark cotton gowns and stuff petticoats, the frocks made to open in front, "so that the little girls could almost dress themselves" (1789).

Low-necked frock of white muslin with high sash 1768–9 (from *Lady Palk and her children* by N. Dance). Detail.

Although dark cottons and printed muslins were worn for every-day and for winter, white muslin with coloured sashes had now become the usual dress wear. A German visitor to London in 1786, wrote of the girls of a school in Queen's Square:

"They all rose and bowed, were all dressed in white and only their unpowdered brown hair and green, red, blue and violet girdles cast a kind of shadow and broke the brilliance: the light white caps lay in neat almost fantastic folds, quite artlessly tied, and the curls in rolls on the prettiest of necks . . . I especially noted (as they danced) their shoes and found that they were fitted to the foot's natural form . . . made like the Turkish slippers men are in the habit of wearing of green red or yellow morocco leather."

(*Sophie in London*, 1933.)

The clothing of a girl at the Blue Coat School, York, in the same year makes an interesting contrast to the dress of these fashionable children, "The wardrobe of every girl whilst she continues in the school consists of the following particulars:

3 pairs of stockings	2 pockets
2 pairs of shoes	2 gowns
2 petticoats	2 bedgowns
2 shifts	2 blue and white aprons
2 pairs of stays	2 aprons
2 nightcaps	1 band or Sunday handkerchief
2 blue and white handkerchiefs	(i.e. for the neck)
2 hats	1 cloak
1 pair of garters	2 pocket handkerchiefs
1 day cap	1 pair of worsted mittens."

At another school, the Bath school attended by Susan Sibbald from 1797–1800, when the girls went to a ball they were all "dressed in book muslin frocks with primrose color'd sashes wide and long and wreaths of roses of the same colour on our heads". A slip of coloured silk was now worn under the almost transparent muslin of the frocks, the word "slip" now referring to a different garment from the "slip" of the middle of the century:

"we were not allowed to appear (in the drawing room) except of an evening when we had to be dressed out for the occasion, in colord silk slips and thin muslin frocks."

(Memoirs of Susan Sibbald.)

By 1800 this style had also become an adult fashion, so that girls and women were once more dressed alike, and a girl born in 1780 wore the same style from babyhood until she was about 30, because her childhood dress had been the forerunner of the new adult fashion.

THE NINETEENTH CENTURY

THE NINETEENTH CENTURY

At the beginning of the century, the *long clothes* worn for the first six or eight months were still influenced by the idea of keeping the child's limbs free, and were much shorter than those which followed. Probably many mothers of 1800 followed the advice given in *The Lady's Monthly Museum* in 1799:

> "with regard to the child's dress in the day—let it be a skirt and petticoat of fine flannel, two or three inches lower than the child's feet, with a dimity top, and this should be made to tie behind; over that a surcingle made of fine buckram, two inches broad, covered with satin or fine ticken with a ribbon fastened to tie it on, which answers every purpose of stays and has none of their inconvenience. Over this put a robe or slip or frock . . . two caps should be put on the head until the child has most of its teeth. . . . Its dress for the night may be a skirt, a blanket to tie on, and then a gown to tie over the blanket."

The long clothes were shortened to three-quarters clothing which was worn for two or three months; then as they began to walk babies were short-coated.

The bare minimum of clothing which a baby was thought to need in 1808 and its plainest form is revealed in the suggestions for the contents of the clothing boxes prepared for "poor lying-in women", given in *The Lady's Economical Assistant*,

Four little shirts
Four little caps
Two frocks
Two little bedgowns
Two flannel blankets
Two rollers
Two pairs of stays and flannel coats
Two upper petticoats
Twenty-four napkins

The shirt, of fine linen or cambric was put on first as it had been beneath the swaddling bands. For some time the shirt kept the eighteenth-century form, open down the front, with the sleeves gathered on the shoulder and with a small gusset beneath the arm, but sleeves were now always open, not gathered into a band, and generally shorter than those of the eighteenth century. The seaming of the shoulders with narrow insertions of lace or openwork continued as well as plain seaming. The flannel blanket, about a yard square of flannel, was worn at night secured by a roller of calico, about 5 inches wide and 1¼ yards long, and the bedgown was worn over this. These garments replaced the daytime wear of frock, upper petticoat, stays of dimity and flannel coat. The term coat was still sometimes used for the under *petticoat*, which was attached to the *stays*. For the children of the poor, upper petticoats of coloured linen matching the frocks of print were recommended. It is only the children of the poor who seem to have worn coloured print frocks from birth. Ladies' children had frocks of muslin, the bodice and skirt set into a narrow band of muslin at the waist and their upper petticoats were of dimity, attached like the flannel petticoat to the stays, "It is a good plan to make button holes in the bands and fix strings or buttons to the stays to fasten the petticoat without pins." The length of the frock was about a yard and for three-quarters clothing this was reduced to about three-quarters of a yard, "but the fullness (about 50 inches) continued while the child is in arms".

All *babies* wore *caps* of linen and muslin, by day and by night, and usually two caps, an undercap and a cap proper. The undercaps were plain, with headpiece and caul, the night-caps were made with cut-out darts sewn into the centre back. The day-caps, an important part of the child's wardrobe, were made and trimmed in a variety of of ways. Foundling caps, which were worn throughout the first half of the century by boys and girls, had the crown shaped by gathering across the back. Many caps were gathered into a small circle of lace, and some had an insertion of lace from this down the centre of the cap, back and front. Most caps had runners, or fine drawstrings, round the headpiece and neck, which were mainly functional, (to adjust the size to the growing child), but were also decorative, "in

PLATE 21

Poor children on left, rich children on right some in scarves
crossed before, one in a long cloak. The girls wear straw hats,
one wears a bonnet, all have elbow-length gloves. 1800.

*Mezzotint "The Sailor's Orphans; or The Young Ladies' Subscription"
by William Ward after William Redmore Bigg
Reproduced by permission of the Syndics of the Fitzwilliam Museum,
Cambridge*

PLATE 22

Little girl, aged 2 years 8 months, in low-necked frock and
cap, her brother, aged 5 years, in skeleton suit with trousers
slit at the ankles. Low laced shoes. 1800.

Archibald and Emma Edmonstone. Henry Edridge (signed and dated.)
Reproduced by kind permission of Commander E. Edmonstone

general the more runners the better". For the poor child the found-ling cap style was recommended, but this too was allowed its narrow edging of lace.

The *frocks* were very simple in form, with a very short bodice, a low neck and short sleeves. In the first years of the century the frocks were often made in a characteristic wrap-over style. The stitching of these small muslin frocks is nearly always exquisitely fine, but the ornament is sparse, narrow muslin frills, narrow insertions and edg-ings of lace or openwork, fine tucking or light embroidery. Susan Sibbald recalled in her *Memoirs* the impression made on her by an over-dressed child of 2 months old, in 1811–12:

"The little infant, which I thought from its being so young would have looked better in its nursery attire of bedgown and nightcap instead of robe and sash and tied-up sleeves, a bare neck and a cap like a sunflower, with a scarlet cockade to match the ribbons of the robe."

For most of the century short sleeves might be tied-up with a ribbon passing under them to tie in a bow outside on the shoulder. At about this time also Fanny Kemble's father apparently indulged in similar parental showing-off:

"My father was convicted during an absence of my mother's from town, of having planted in my baby bosom the seeds of personal vanity, while indulging his own, by having an especially pretty and becoming lace cap at hand in the drawing room, to be immediately substituted for some more homely adornment, when I was exhibited to visitors."

c. 1810. (*Records of a Girlhood*, F. A. Kemble, 1878.)

The noblest and wealthiest babies had to suffer a great smothering of lace on state occasions. The child who became the fourth Marquess of Londonderry, had a layette which cost nearly £2,000 and for which, "Paris, Brussels, London and Vienna had been ransacked" in 1821. For poorer children one simply-cut style served for frock, flannel, petticoat and bedgown alike. Miss Mitford, in *Our Village*, gives a glimpse of village babies of the 1820s,

"There it sits in all the dignity of the baby adorned in a pink-checked frock or a blue-spotted pinafore and in a little white cap tolerably clean and quite whole. One is forced to ask if it be a boy or girl; for these hardy country rogues are all alike, open-eyed, weather-stained and nothing fearing."

By the 1820s the first shirts, still open down the front, were cut so that the top, back and front, folded down over the bodice of the flannel. Stays no longer appear in the baby's first clothing in the 1830s, but because "infants require warmth and support round the stomach and hips" they wore a flannel band about 31½ inches long and 5½ inches wide for the first ten or twelve months, wound round them. There were different styles of flannel gowns but one which was in general use from the 1820s to the end of the century was a straight piece of flannel—for which the term *blanket* was still often used—with sewn down pleats to the waist, hollowed out at the top for the arms, with the binding carried over the shoulder to form straps, and tied with pairs of tapes down the back. This preserved the style of the eighteenth-century christening robe. Another style had a bodice with a long end to thread through a slit and a wrap-over skirt which tied at the side, a style which was still being used at the end of the century. *Pilches* or "savers" to prevent the clothes from being wetted were made from a square of flannel, and bibs, three or four folds of diaper, were "often used . . . when cutting teeth". *Socks or boots* of knitted wool or cotton were worn. The *nightgowns*, loose and full had long sleeves and were gathered at the front under the centre of their waistband. This form hardly varied for the rest of the century.

For the first three months of its life the baby of the 1830s was carried about in a square of flannel, and there were also fine knitted shawls, "a zephyr, a soft shawl, to lay a baby in", but after that, for outdoor wear it had a cloak or pelisse of flannel or merino. A *hood* was put on over the day-cap, merino or kerseymere, lined with silk. A rosette on the hood revealed the sex of the child:

"a rosette of satin ribbon is worn on the left side if a boy, and in front, if a girl".

(*The Workwoman's Guide, 1838.*)

For the christening the mantle could be very elaborate. A baby of 1836 had one of

> "white satin covered in Indian muslin . . . five yards of faultless white satin. It must be of a most luscious article, soft as down, with a soupcon of pink blush on it. . . . It must be trimmed either with silk fringe or swansdown."
>
> *(Caroline Clive, 1949.)*

Caps were still worn until about 1850. The foundling shape was still used for day and night wear. Caps for babies of the poor, in soft calico or checked muslin, were usually of this style, or a folded rectangle, shaped by drawstrings. The caps of more fortunate babies were of lawn or cambric with muslin frills and lace edgings. For day-caps the muslin itself was often embroidered and caps had generally become more elaborate. The lace or embroidered cap crowns were large, two or three inches across, or sometimes horse-shoe shaped. Embroidery and lace were often set off by an undercap of pink, blue or white satin. After 1850 ideas about babies wearing caps indoors changed:

> "Caps with their trimming of three or four rows of lace and large cockades which rivalled in size the dear little round face of the child are now discontinued almost entirely within doors, though the poor child is still overwhelmed with cap, hat and feathers in its daily airing."
>
> *(Dress as a Fine Art*, Mrs. Merrifield, 1854.)

According to Dr. Walsh, in *The Manual of Domestic Economy*, 1856, the reason for this was, "experience teaching that the head is a part which is much better kept at as low a temperature as the room ought to be where the baby is. . . ." A cap continued to be worn under the hood when the baby was taken out of doors and head squares of flannel were used, "to throw over the infant's head when going from room to room" (*Englishwoman's Domestic Magazine*, 1868). These still appeared in lists of baby clothing in the 1890s.

Apart from the absence of the caps, the clothing recommended by Dr. Walsh in 1856 showed little change in the type and number of garments worn by the new-born child:

"an outer garment, variously ornamented and named either a nightgown, daygown or robe; two flannel articles . . . called long flannels and barrows;" (? one night and day or both together); "the shirt next the skin; a swathe for effecting a certain amount of pressure on the navel; diaper napkin and flannel square . . . very fine cambric or lawn is the proper material to be placed next to the skin".

A *barrow* was a piece of flannel wrapped round below the arms, the part extending beyond the feet, being turned up and pinned.

Lawn and cambric shirts, now also called *chemises* were made in the same style for a third generation. Sometimes the flaps were rounded and the shoulders made to turn back over the top of the arm, a style worn throughout the second half of the century. The wide open sleeve with gathering at the top of the shoulder no longer appeared after the middle of the century. This sleeve was replaced by a very short one, little more than a band for lace, and sometimes

Baby's first (open) shirt and second (closed) shirt. (E. Roseveare, *Textbook of Needlework* . . . 1895).

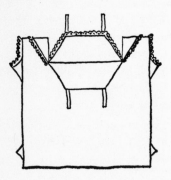

there was lace or embroidery only, lifted into a sleeve by a small gusset at the base. Some shirts have a broad-based sleeve, giving an upward slant to the opening, "easier to tie up", others have a small sleeve cut in one with the body. Only rarely were the shoulders still joined with insertions.

Throughout the century the *gowns* catch a little of the changing forms of fashion and the changing styles of ornament. The simplicity of the earlier gowns was replaced by more elaborate shaping of the sleeve, which was puffed in accordance with the styles of the 1820s and 1830s. This full puffing disappeared in the 1840s when the sleeve was very short and narrow. The bodice grew longer and was much enriched with embroidery and the skirt grew longer, fuller and more important and was also often embroidered:

> "Infant robes are, as usual, plain and simple in form; but they are frequently very richly ornamented with needlework or lace."
> (*Lady's Newspaper*, 1850.)

The needlework which most often ornamented the robes at this time, particularly the christening robes, was the fine white embroidery known as Ayrshire work. This embroidery of raised satin stitch with needlepoint fillings, worked in delicate flower and feathery leaf patterns, formed a stomacher panel on the bodice and a panel widening from waist to hem on the skirt. It was much used for robes of the middle of the century, 1830 to 1870, although many of these were used again for succeeding generations.

Embroidery and lace and their arrangement on the gowns reflect the current fashions. By 1870 the gowns showed the princess line in the panel of ornament, which tapered at the waist but swept without break there from neck to hem:

> "the princess robe, now much favoured as it permits of such fancy trimming down the entire front, but bodice and skirt also used."
> (*Weldon's Practical Baby Clothing, c.* 1885.)

Insertions of lace alternated with bands of puffed muslin across this panel, and, towards the end of the century lace and embroidery, alternated with fine tucking.

These were the robes of ceremony. For everyday wear the gowns were more simple, "few ladies now dress their infants in lavishly trimmed and embroidered robes", said the *Englishwoman's Domestic Magazine* in 1868, in recommending a pattern for a monthly gown with a sleeve which could be turned into a short sleeve to make the gown a day gown. The term *monthly gown* was used from the 1850s for the long-sleeves gowns which were worn for day and night during the first month and were identical with the nightgowns in their style.

Out of doors *cloaks* of merino and cashmere, trimmed with silk fringe or swansdown were worn in the 1840s and 1850s, but borders of quilted satin were also fashionable in the 1850s and this type of ornament continued in cloaks of the 1860s and 1870s. The cloak by then was often a single, circular cape but the older style with cape and collar, that is a three-tiered cloak, was still worn. Cashmere remained the usual material, white, grey, crimson, scarlet or blue, with white silk lining and facings of matching or contrasting silk; lining and facing might both be quilted. By the 1880s the quilted facings were becoming old-fashioned and were replaced by borders of embroidery. In cold weather a knitted jacket was sometimes worn beneath the cloak. *Veils* of fine Shetland wool were used to protect the face in the 1860s, but by the 1880s, wool was no longer regarded as suitable for this purpose.

By the middle of the century the freedom which babies had enjoyed at the beginning of the century had lessened, mainly owing to the increased length and fullness of the robe, which involved not only the greater length of material in the robe itself, but additional material in the flannel and petticoat beneath it. In 1838, although the length given in *The Workwoman's Guide* for long clothes was 40½ inches, and for children of the poor, who always seem to have the advantage here, 36 inches, the lengths for flannel gowns was 1 yard and about 30 inches, with the comment, "some ladies dress their children in very long flannels and robes, but this is as unnecessary as it is ill-judged". But the lengths of gowns and their fullness increased during the 1840s and 1850s.

"The long petticoats are as absurd as they are prejudicial to the child. The evil has of late years rather increased than diminished, for the clothes are not only made much longer but much fuller, so that the poor victim has an additional weight to bear . . . many instances can be mentioned in which the long clothes have been made a yard and a quarter long."

(*Dress as a Fine Art*, 1854.)

In the late 1860s, in *Cassell's Household Guide*, it is stated that:

"robes which once reached absurd proportions are curtailed to the length of a yard", but it is pointed out that "the length of the skirt of a robe thirty or forty years ago was 40 inches and the body three inches. A full dress robe is now made 36 inches long in the skirt and five in the body."

Although everyday robes might be plain in the skirt, the "best" robes gave ample opportunity for a combined display of maternal pride and paternal affluence. Full dress robes of the 1870s and 1880s were still about 45 inches long. The display of them could only be seen to advantage if the child were carried in the arms of mother or nurse. When a new type of baby carriage appeared in the 1880s, "the larger, safer and more comfortable four-wheeled carriage for one or two children in which babies can either sit up and enjoy a good view of the world around them, or lie down and sleep as comfortably as if they were in their own snug little beds at home" (*Myra's Journal*, 1884), the practice of carrying babies out of doors was gradually abandoned. The period for wearing long clothes and the long clothes themselves alike were shortened. The stage of three-quarters clothing was also being gradually abandoned.

An article in *The Queen* in 1879 criticised the contemporary dress of children on several points:

"the clothing of infants is usually linen or cotton with very little flannel, and none next to the skin, the arms and chest are almost invariably exposed and insufficiently covered; the legs, ankles and feet are also naked. Tightness in the bandages, bodices and stays constitutes a common evil, and last of all we have the absurd fashion of long petticoats, usually stiffly starched and weighing down the infant's body. The flannel petticoat as at present worn is an excellent garment and the only fault . . . too low in the neck and long in the skirt. A dress cut high in the neck and long in the sleeves and extending six or seven inches below the feet only is recommended, cutting out the stage of 'shortening'; and the wearing of a flannel shirt for winter as soon as the child is old enough and cotton next to the skin at night."

The length recommended is, however, still longer than the length recommended in 1799, which was "two or three inches longer than the child's feet".

Linen or cambric shirts had been worn as the first garment next to the skin by so many generations of babies that, although vests or jackets of flannel had been recommended for children a little older, since the 1830s, especially if they were delicate, it was not until the end of the century that flannel *vests* began to be worn by babies. The opinion that cambric was better for a baby's tender skin was, however, still held, and linen and cambric shirts were still in use at

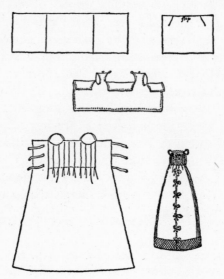

Baby's first shirt; flannel ,and "handsome
day flannel", with quilted bodice and hem
(*Cassell's Household Guide I, c.* 1870)

PLATE 23

Two boys in short low-necked frocks with short trousers
showing below. Baby in short dress, wearing cap. *c.* 1810.

H. Edridge
Reproduced by kind permission of Messrs. Appleby Bros., 10 Ryder Street,
London

PLATE 24

Small boys in short jackets, pantaloons and shoes with shoe-
laces. Both have tall hats. 1811.

the end of the century. Knitted woollen vests were also just beginning to be worn at the end of the century.

Although the corded stays of the beginning of the century were
no longer worn the bodice of the day flannel was often quilted and
the flannel bands had increased in length by the middle of the century. They had also increased in stiffness.

> "Another evil practice which some years since prevailed universally
> was that of rolling a bandage three inches in width and two or three
> yards in length round the body of the child."
>
> (*Dress as a Fine Art*, 1854.)

In a child's book, published in the same year, *The Diary of a Baby
Boy*, by E. Berger, there is an account of his nurse undressing him
and preparing him for the night:

> "Nurse . . . put on its nightcap with the pretty little frill, and she
> took off its roller—such many, many times she turned the baby to
> pull off the long roller! And then she drew off its dear little shirt.
> . . . Then Willy held its nightgown to the fire while it was being
> washed . . . when she had tied on the night gown she wrapped the
> baby up altogether in a white shawl which mamma had worked
> herself."

The tradition of swaddling bands was a very strong one. The soft
flannel had also been replaced to some extent by linen webbing;
"some ladies prefer these of flannel, but there is more support in the
webbing" (*Englishwoman's Domestic Magazine*, 1868). Flannel had
returned to favour again by the 1870s and the length was reduced
to a band of flannel about 30 inches by $4\frac{1}{2}$ inches wound twice
round the child, and its length gradually reduced, or a flannel *binder*.
Knitted bands were also recommended during the 1880s and 1890s,
but the stouter binders continued in use as well as the flannel ones
until the end of the century. Knitted pilches were also worn.

Waterproof pilches had appeared in the 1860s but were doubt-
fully received on the grounds of their not being healthy. But an
invention of 1878, "the new-fashioned safety pin with a solid guard
to cover the point" was generally welcomed as a safe fastener for
napkins. Up to this time they had been fastened by loops and

Baby's Pilch knitted in white wool, white Peacock fingering. 1886–8. (*Weldon's Practical Knitter.*)

buttons, or by ordinary pins, though this was not generally approved.

A set of long clothing given in *The Lady's World*, 1899, "in order of putting on" is very little different from that given in *The Work-woman's Guide* of sixty years before: flannel binder 6 inches by 27 inches; day shirt of cambric with flaps and open in front; long flannel skirt 1 yard long, "turned up and pinned over the feet"; linen binder of stout twill; long white petticoat; robe. For outdoor wear there is a pelisse in cream wool with a cape, trimmed with swansdown and a bonnet of tucked silk, also trimmed with swansdown, and with lace. The nightgown has long sleeves and there are also several rather ornamental bibs. With the restricting binder of stout linen twill as well as the flannel one worn next to the skin the baby of 1899 would have been more tightly bound than the baby of 1838. The length of the two flannels is the same. But this baby clothing on the eve of the twentieth century is far longer, fuller, more constricting and more overwhelming than the clothing recommended for the baby of just a hundred years earlier.

Short coating

When a child was about 9 months old its first open shirt was changed for a closed shirt. Sometimes this was simply the first shirt sewn up:

> "when the babe is short-coated it may either wear the little chemise it has already worn joined up the back, or have a set of six new ones". (*Cassell's Household Guide, c.* 1870.)

The second shirts differed from the first in having no opening down the front, or back—they seem sometimes to have been worn that way—but they often have little vents with gussets at the bottom, like a man's shirt. For the whole of the middle period of the century they followed the style of the first shirts in having flaps back and front to fold down over the stays. The shoulder piece was often shaped or slit to turn back over the straps of stays or petticoat bodice and sometimes, trimmed to turn out over the frock. The flaps often had tapes to tie them down under the arms. This style was worn until about the age of 6, when for girls it merged into the adult chemise, made with gores, and for boys into a form closer to that of a man's shirt. An alternative style more like the adult chemise was already appearing in the 1860s. When the style of the shirt changed the open flannel gown was changed for one with a sewn-up skirt on a bodice. By 1838 simple, sleeveless nightvests of flannel were sometimes worn instead of, or beneath, the linen shirt. Delicate children were recommended to wear in the daytime too, "flannel shirts or vests next to the skin cut in much the same shape as babies second shirts, but no sleeves and back hollowed out". By the second half of the century little jackets of Welsh flannel were worn beneath the shirt by many children between the ages of 1 and 3 years, whether delicate or not, all the year round.

At the beginning of the century stays of corded material, 9 inches long, were recommended for children of 2. Stays of jean or linen, corded or later quilted, fastening with tapes or made with one long end to pass through a slit to meet the other in front, where they tied, became a little shorter by the middle of the century, about 5 inches long. The next size, for children of 2 or 3 was then about 7 or 8 inches. The stays were generally no more than the corded bodice of the flannel petticoat. The petticoat was sewn on to the bodice for children of about 1 year old, but from 2 or 3 it was buttoned to the stays, which then had one row of buttons for drawers and another row above for the petticoat. This method persisted to the end of the century. The upper petticoat of cotton was, throughout the century made on a bodice, changing slightly in its shaping, to meet the shape of the frock. The petticoat of the 1830s still had a short bodice and its short sleeves were now puffed; in the middle years of the century the bodice was longer, with short, tight sleeves or no sleeves at all,

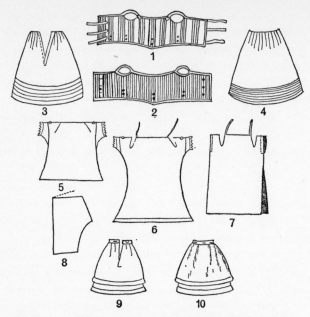

Baby's second shirt, or chemise (5). Child of two or three:
stays (1, 2); petticoat (3, 4); chemise (6), boy's shirt (7);
drawers (8); flannel petticoat (9, 10). (*Cassell's Household
Guide I, c.* 1870.)

and a much fuller skirt. This remained a general pattern although in
the late 1870s and early 1880s there were princess petticoats without
fullness for the princess frocks. Knitted woollen petticoats were also
made, especially for delicate children, because they were lighter.

In the 1880s Ada S. Ballin, who edited the late nineteenth-century
journal, *Baby*, recommended that when "they begin to walk"
children should wear all-woollen clothing, next to the skin a long-
sleeved, high-necked vest, over this a high-necked flannel bodice
with or without sleeves, to which the drawers and petticoats should
be buttoned, or a combination garment, with a woollen petticoat
buttoned on to it. Over this the dress should be high in the neck
with long sleeves and reach nearly to the ankles, "charming little
dresses for small children can be knitted or crochetted out of thick
Berlin wool" (*Science of Dress*, 1885). The union or combination

Baby's petticoat with bodice, knitted in
white and red Berlin fingering. 1888.
(*Weldon's Practical Knitter.*)

garment, later known as *combinations*—chemise and drawers combined—was adopted for children during the 1880s, though generally
not until they were 2 or 3. There is an earlier example of this combined garment, probably 1820–30, in the Museum of Costume at
Bath.

At the beginning of the century, boys and girls, when fully on
their feet, wore *pantaloons*, not petticoats beneath their frocks, with
drawers beneath these, flannel in winter, calico in summer:

> "It is now so much the fashion to dress children, both boys and girls
> in pantaloons instead of petticoats."
> (*The Lady's Economical Assistant*, 1808.)

The *drawers* were set into a band to button on to the stays and
were open except for the lower part of the leg. The pantaloons or
trousers were a little longer, reaching the ankle and were usually
closed in the legs and up the front with the centre back seam open or
short slits from the waist each side; sometimes they were on a bodice
with straps to go over the shoulders. At the beginning of the century
children just beginning to walk, who may be boys or girls, are shown
with frocks to the knees and no trousers, but generally boys of 2 and
3 wore *trousers* with knee-length frocks from about 1805 onwards.
Girls of this age have frocks to the ankle, too long to reveal whether
they are wearing trousers or not, until the second decade of the century, when their encased legs are visible beneath shorter frocks.

C.C.E.–L

During the 1820s and 1830s, boys, as long as they wore frocks, and girls continued to show these trousers as part of their dress. Up to this time trousers were fairly plain, but during the 1840s and 1850s they grew wider, with deep frills of embroidery, and then shortened until the frills were all that showed. By the 1860s the frills too were disappearing from sight, and trousers were now completely an undergarment and known as drawers, made with the legs gathered into a band at the knee with a narrow frill of embroidery, seamed at the back and front, with opening at the sides.

Throughout the country the first *short frocks* were generally of muslin or cambric. In 1822 the little boy who was the excuse for the costly layette mentioned above,* now a year and 7 months old, paid a visit to the Austrian Empress, dressed in:

> "a cambric frock with blue ribbons let in down the robings (the frills down bodice and skirt, suggesting a robe), trimmed with lace and hanging buttons. His trousers were three rows of lace, his stockings *à jour* and little black shoes, a broad light blue sash and shoulder knots and his hair nicely settled."

His sister, about 8 months old, had:

> "a cambric worked frock, blue satin sash and shoulder knots and a beautiful cap, lined and trimmed with blue, blue necklace and bracelets."
>
> (*Frances Anne, . . . Marchioness of Londonderry*, 1958.)

About four months later they went to see Marie-Louise of Parma. Henry then wore a pink silk frock and his trousers were not mentioned, Fanny a muslin embroidered frock over a pink petticoat with cap to match and a pink necklace.

Muslin and silk were worn for dress occasions, but nankeen, holland and prints were used for everyday. Thin woollen fabrics made warmer frocks for winter.

Some of the simpler frocks were cut in one piece, but most were made with a skirt and bodice joined at the waist, fastening down the back. The bodice gradually grew longer during the 1820s and until the 1850s. Short sleeves were general, but when long sleeves were worn, as they were in the 1820s and 1830s, they showed something

* See p. 149

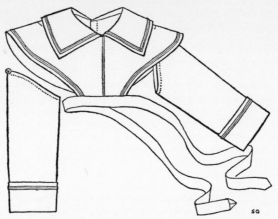

Fawn cotton tippet and sleeves, 1820–30. (Gallery of English Costume, Manchester. Drawn by S. Gregory.)

of the fashionable shape. Because of the low necks and short sleeves, spencers were worn out of doors from the beginning of the century until the 1840s. The *spencer* was like the dress bodice, with long sleeves high neck and collar and, unlike the adult spencer, this also fastened at the back. Children also wore tippets and sleeves—short capes with sleeves attached—to cover the bare neck and arms. Dresses sometimes had detachable long sleeves to button on to short ones.

The plain muslin frocks were high-waisted and generally lightly embroidered at the beginning of the century. In the 1820s and 1830s the skirts widened and there were frills and embroidery at the hem. Muslin and print dresses of the 1830s were piped and often trimmed with fine braid. More elaborate dresses were lavishly embroidered in the fine white work of the 1830s and 1840s and this in turn was replaced by the larger openwork, broderie anglaise, which was particularly popular on frocks of muslin and cotton, for children between the ages of 1 and 3. A child of 2 or 3 might wear in 1847:

"a dress of white cambric muslin, embroidered up the front *en tablier*, that is to say the embroidery widens from the waist to the feet, a double row of needlework set on at the sides so as to turn back on the dress. A round pelerine (i.e. a short cape), black silk mittens blue chequered ribbon sash, bow and long ends behind, black glazed leather shoes."

(*Lady's Newspaper*, 1847.)

All these dresses were made low in the neck and with short sleeves and were usually worn with shoulder knots and sashes of coloured ribbon, the sash being either round the waist or over one shoulder. When trousers were disappearing from the legs, the dresses remained at knee level and fanned out over fuller petticoats:

"no sooner than they can walk the petticoats are so shortened that they scarcely cover the child's back when it stoops".

(*Dress as a Fine Art*, 1854.)

By the middle of the century warmer materials were general for the winter months, "for dresses intended to supercede the long robe, cashmere is a favoured material and it may be ornamented with embroidery, worked in a light wreath pattern above a deep hem. To these cashmere dresses is frequently added a little pardessus of the same material" (*Lady's Newspaper*, 1850). The *pardessus*, a short jacket, usually with open sleeves now took the place of the spencer.

Until they were 2 or 3 years old boys wore frocks not very

Frock for a boy or girl, *broderie anglaise* on cambric. (*Englishwoman's Domestic Magazine*, 1857.)

different from those of little girls. A wrap-over front fastening,
slantwise from top to bottom, or slantwise trimming, was sometimes
used for boys' frocks, instead of the usual back fastening. During the
early 1860s boys' dresses had flat pleats in the skirt, but by the late
1860s when frocks generally were "completely gored on both sides
of the front breadth which is set into the body perfectly plain at the
waist", boys' frocks, but not girls', were gored a little each side of
the back as well. The skirts were now about 18 inches long and the
bodices 8 inches deep on the first short frocks (*Cassell's Household
Guide, c. 1870*). Velvet was a favourite material for these small
frocks. For a boy of 2 in 1862, "a pretty little blue velvet dress . . .
made with a low body, cut square, trimmed round with handsome
open embroidery" was thought suitable. The hat to be worn with

Short coating. (*a*) dress for boy or girl (*b, d*) for
girl (*c*) for boy (*e*) pelisse (*f*) paletot. (*Cassell's
Household Guide, I, c, 1870.*)

this was also in blue velvet, trimmed with a blue-tipped, white feather (*Englishwoman's Domestic Magazine*, 1862). Plaid and striped woollen materials and poplin were also much in favour in the 1860s, "for a little boy, two and a half years old, a frock of red and white striped poplin, low square bodice and short sleeves, trimmed with black velvet ribbon and small gimp buttons. The skirt is quite plain in front . . . there are pleats at the side and back" (ibid., 1866). White embroidered collars and sleeve edgings were added to dresses of wool, silk, poplin and velvet. A large proportion of these frocks have low necks and short sleeves and leave the shoulders completely exposed.

By the late 1870s even dresses as small as these showed the prevailing influence of the princess line. A dress for an infant in 1880 was "cut plain back and front and trimmed with work to form its style" (*Ladies Treasury*), that is, like the women's dresses at the time it was composed of trimmings, pleated flounces, puffed plastron, on a lining. In 1887 *The Lady's World* said, "Fine work, insertion, ribbon, appear indispensable for dresses worn by children up to the age of two or three years." The very low necks and short sleeves were now disappearing from the first short frocks, at least in winter, "I hope there are few women who dress their babies in low-necked and short-sleeved frocks in the winter" (*Woman's World*, 1888). By the 1890s the elaborate frocks of the 1880s were replaced by a simpler style falling from a yoke free or gathered to a low waist.

There are references to *crawlers* or clothes protectors from the middle of the century. George du Maurier, writing to his mother in 1865 spoke of Tricksy walking unaided across the nursery on her first birthday, "she wears a huge pair of knickerbockers over her petticoats to keep them clean, her appearance is very comical" (*The Young George du Maurier*, D. du Maurier, 1951). A pattern and description were given in *Weldon's Practical Baby Clothing*, c. 1885.

As soon as they began to walk, children wore *pinafores* over their frocks to keep them clean. Early in the century these were called pincloths and seem generally to have been plain and simple covers with a drawstring at the neck and an opening down the back, in holland, linen, print or muslin. Some have narrow edgings of open-

work embroidery round the neck and armholes, and by the 1820s and
1830s, if not earlier, had the front gathered at the centre beneath a
strip of insertion continuing as loose plain strings, to tie at the back,
as in a baby's nightgown. Some of the pinafores had lappets at the
shoulder to protect the short sleeves, in the 1830s when the sleeves
were full. The pinafore replaced the apron in children's dress, but the
apron still survived for a short time in the early nineteenth century.
There is an example of a very practical device, an apron of the same
material as the frock, in the Gallery of English Costume, Manchester,
from the 1820s. The small pinafores of the middle of the century
were still often the plain flat shape, but also are made with the attached waistband. By the 1860s some have curved fronts and backs and
others have the back ending at the waist. The most popular material
for them seems to have been a fine linen of diaper weave, known
by this name, a strong fabric with excellent washing qualities, edged,
first with muslin frills or narrow openwork, later with lace or crochet

Pinafore; pinafore frock without belt or trimming,
belt and finished pinafore frock; fitting paletot; for girl
of 8. (*Cassell's Household Guide III, c.* 1870.)

edgings. Brown holland edged with blue or scarlet braid was also a popular material after children were about 18 months old, "The holland pinafore may be worn over winter frocks and alone in summer" (*Cassell's Household Guide, c.* 1870). The less enveloping dress pinafores which developed in the 1870s were sometimes so decorative that their original purpose disappears. An infant's pinafore, in 1883, was made of cambric, "closed at each side with bows for the frock to show beneath" (*Ladies Treasury*). Pinafores of the 1890s had yokes of lace and insertion and embroidery frills at the shoulders for sleeves.

Socks were generally white wool or cotton, hand or machine-knitted. Fashionably dressed children might wear socks of patterned openwork. By the 1880s although socks were still general children of about 2 might wear stockings, often black or brown. The first *shoes* were generally of cloth or silk tied over the instep and there was little change in this first style during the century. Knitted boots and drawers combined were sometimes worn.

> "As soon as it begins to get about on its feet, let it have little shoes . . . very small pieces of silk, merino or llama will make a baby's quilted shoes. Many ladies make such shoes for fancy bazaars. When the child begins to walk, let it have easy black kid. shoes with straps."
>
> (*Cassell's Household Guide, c.* 1870.)

The tie style was worn by children up to the age of 4 until the

Baby's boots and leggings combined. 1886. (*Weldon's Practical Knitter.*)

1840s, when shoes with an ankle strap became the general fashion
for the second shoe and remained the usual style for children of about
2 to 4 until the end of the century. Red, blue and white shoes were
worn by children as well as black and bronze. Short boots of cloth
or kid with side buttoning were also worn from the 1840s, elastic-
sided boots from the middle of the century, followed by front
buttoning and front lacing styles in the 1870s and 1880s, but boots
were less popular in the 1890s for small children.

Outdoors small children wore a *pelisse*. For most of the century
this was a coat with a cape, sometimes attached, sometimes separate.
The style varied only a little in accordance with the fashionable line,
but its trimmings usually reflected current fashion. The pelisses of
the 1830s were, in spite of their sleeves, rather cape-like in shape;
later pelisses were cut more like frocks of the time, but unlike these
always had a high neck and long sleeves and front fastening. A
pelisse was put on instead of a frock when the child went out of
doors, although in cold weather both were worn. As soon as the
child started to walk the pelisse was shortened from full-length to
"halfway between the sock and the top of the boot" (ibid.) but by
the 1890s they were again a little longer. The long cape which had
made the pelisse a distinctive garment was disappearing by the end

Small boy in braided jacket, waistcoat and
skirt, wearing socks and button boots; and
holding a straw hat. 1868. (From an original
photograph).

of the century, when small children wore a coat or sometimes a cape as the first outer garment after long clothes. Short jackets were also worn in the middle of the century, though "less ladylike than pelisses" (ibid.), and the frock had always to be worn beneath. But many dresses surviving from 1850–80 have been made with matching jackets. The most popular fabrics were merino for winter and various cotton fabrics for summer, nankeen and dimity in the early part of the century, piqué in the middle period and figured cottons towards the end. Fine muslins were also used and "stuff", which usually meant the cheaper woollen fabrics. Plush, a favourite material of the 1880s, was then used for children's as for women's garments. Black velveteen, brown and blue merino and blue poplin were the colours recommended in the late 1860s, but pelisses in white, cream, pale-grey or fawn were more usual. The merino pelisses of the 1850s were trimmed with silk fringe, cotton ones with embroidery or braid. During the 1860s braiding was general and in the 1870s and 1880s there were deep flounces and insertions of embroidery or lace and borders of silk embroidery. In the 1890s the yoke construction of

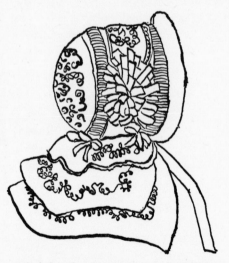

Baby's hood, white satin, trimmed with silk braid and ribbon. (*Lady's Newspaper*, 1851.)

dresses appeared also in the pelisse and the trimming outlined the yoke, or a short ornamental cape or capes, fell over a plain yoke.

The hood was left off with the long clothes, at least by little boys. Girls wore soft *bonnets* which generally showed some influence of the fashionable bonnet of the time, but, as they kept a deep curtain, were still hood-like,

> "the first bonnet after the hood should be soft, warm and, till they are two or three, cloth, merino, silk, satin, print or calico, in preference to straw or pasteboard".
>
> (*The Workwoman's Guide*, 1838.)

Boys, on the other hand, wore a series of *hats*. In the 1830s a square crown with a turned-up brim with a rosette was popular and during the 1840s and 1850s round hats with medium high crowns:

> "Boys (of two to four) usually wear round straw hats turned up at the brim or fancy caps."
>
> (*Lady's Newspaper*, 1850.)

The straw hats were often trimmed with a feather and cockades of ribbon. In the 1860s a small round hat, with turned-up brim in velvet or felt was popular and was regarded as "the best shape to carry an infant in" (*Englishwoman's Domestic Magazine*, 1862). Straw hats were worn in summer. Feathers were the usual trimming, long and drooping in the 1840s and 1850s, but by the 1860s often in tufts or cockades, "tufts or cockades more in favour than long feathers" (ibid., 1861–2). The small round hat was worn throughout the 1860s; little boys of 2 years old wore hats "of the turban or pork pie

Boy's straw hat, lined and trimmed with blue silk and ribbon. (*Lady's Newspaper*, 1850.)

shape . . . a short curled white feather under a bow or rosette"
(*Cassell's Household Guide*, c. 1870). The changing ideas of the 1880s
regarded these hats which did not protect the ears as harmful, "It is
terrible to see baby boys going out with their ears exposed to these
bitter east winds" (*Woman's World*, 1888) and advocated the general
use of hoods. Hoods were not, however, generally popular for small
boys of walking age. The bonnets of small girls of the same age were
frilled elaborately round the face or high on the head during the
1880s and 1890s. Hats for boys and girls alike grew larger in the
1880s and generally had turned-up brims; in the 1890s the brims
grew wider and as the hats were often worn well back on the head
this brim framed the face in a large halo. Girls, particularly in
summer, wore this shape in soft frilled and ruched materials, which
made an elaborate frame to the face. Boys' hats were generally
stiffer and sometimes the wide brim was cocked a little and the hat
trimmed with a feather.

.   .   .

Boys' Clothes

Small boys, up to the age of 4, now wore frocks, with trousers to
the ankles. Their next garment was the *skeleton suit*. This, already
worn since the 1780s, was to remain popular until the 1830s. It had
passed out of fashion when Dickens, who would have worn one
himself as a boy, set down, in *Sketches from Boz* (1838–9), this description of it:

> "a skeleton suit, one of those straight blue cloth cases in which small
> boys used to be confined before belts and tunics had come in . . .
> an ingenious contrivance for displaying the symmetry of a boy's
> figure by fastening him into a very tight jacket, with an ornamental
> row of Buttons over each shoulder and then buttoning his trousers
> over it so as to give his legs the appearance of being hooked on just
> under the arm-pits".

From about the age of 7 the boy wore the short *jacket* outside the
trousers, and the "hooked on" appearance of the legs disappeared.
The jacket was still very short. At the beginning of the century some
jackets still had a short pleated tail, but the round jacket soon became

Skeleton suit, fawn cotton, with detach-
able long sleeves, 1800–10. (Gallery of
English Costume, Manchester. Drawn by
S. Gregory.)

the more general form and the tailed form disappeared from the
dress of young boys. The fronts of the round jackets either buttoned
up to the neck or turned back in lapels. For older boys the lapels were
often deep and showed the fashionable **M** notch between lapel and
collar. At the waist the jacket might be shaped to a point. This style
was known as a hussar jacket, "my friend the little hussar", wrote
Miss Mitford, of an 8-year-old boy in *Our Village*, "I do not know
his name and call him after his hat and jacket." Both the skeleton
suit and the round jackets were styles worn by boys only. Boys over
the age of 12 might appear in adult styles, "If any Boys wear round
jackets she had much rather his (Willy's, son of William Words-
worth, born 1810) was made in that form as he looks such a little
old man with flaps." (1821.) (*Letters of Sarah Hutchinson*, 1800–35,
1954.)

Trousers at the beginning of the century, particularly for the smaller boys, were narrow and rather short, often with an ankle slit, but they were less often skin-tight than they had been in the 1790s, and they tended to become wide gradually but steadily during the first half of the century. By the 1820s the ankle slits had gone and the trousers were often strapped under the foot. They had either full-falls or half-falls, until the 1830s, when fly fronts were becoming general, "Boys' trousers are worn close-fitting at the waist and hips but easy in the legs with a fly in front and strapped down under the boot or shoe" (J. Couts, *A Practical Guide for the Tailor's Cutting Room*, *c.* 1843). By 1849 the trousers had become looser, "like sailors' trousers", and "trousers with fullness at the top in the manner of sailors" (*Lady's Newspaper*, 1849).

Trousers and jacket were often in contrasting colours; a blue or red jacket with fawn or white trousers was particularly popular. They were in cloth, nankeen or drill. A single- or double-breasted *waistcoat* was often worn, usually buttoning high at the beginning of the century, with deeper lapels by the 1820s, especially for older

Schoolboy in tail coat, 1816. (From a print of
Reading School, by E. Havell.)

boys. The *waistcoat* was of matching or contrasting cloth, or often in a stout cotton dimity. The jackets usually opened at the cuffs, with one or two buttons, and had ornamental rows of buttons each side of the front opening, to the shoulder, making three rows altogether over the small area of the fronts. The length of the jacket increased slightly during the 1820s and 1830s.

At the beginning of the century the white linen *shirt collar*, edged with a muslin frill spread over the top of the jacket. By 1815, jacket and waistcoat were buttoning higher and the area of visible shirt was lessening. Many small boys, in high-buttoning jackets showed only a frill round the neck. For older boys the frilled collar disappeared altogether and a plain linen collar folded over the top of the jacket was worn. After the 1820s the ruff-like frill of small boys also disappeared. The collar, sometimes still with a frilled edge for younger boys then spread out again, this time wide over the shoulder and closed at the front, showing the same form as women's collars of this time. It was held by a wide ribbon bow or loosely knotted silk handkerchief at the opening. Older boys wore the collar raised by a black cravat, in the adult fashion. During the 1840s the collar grew smaller, and the frilled front was being replaced by an opening set in a pleated and stitched panel. The collar on a small boy's shirt might be embroidered.

Nightshirts were worn and continued to be used until the end of the century, although *pyjamas* were just beginning to come into use in the last year or two. *Night-caps* were worn until the 1830s. A style of night-cap recommended for a child of 2 years of age was also recommended as a style for schoolboys in *The Lady's Economical Assistant*, 1808, "this cap being double throughout is very excellent for boys at school, and may easily be made larger". After a visit of inspection to the Charity Hospital at Bedford, in 1815, the Committee reported that the pillows were very greasy because no night-caps were allowed. Three years later things had improved, but they then recommended that the boys should be allowed two clean shirts a week instead of one (Minute Books, Harpur Trust, 1764–1833, B.R.O.*). The underwear that a boy was expected to take to

* Beds. County Record Office.

Charterhouse School in 1826 was "eight shirts, six pairs of worsted stockings, six pairs of cotton stockings, six pocket handkerchiefs, three nightshirts, three nightcaps" (B.R.O.,★ DD.GA. 48).

Stockings were usually white or cream during the first half of the century, although small boys also wore plaid stockings in the 1840s. Shoes had flat heels and tied over the instep; short boots were also worn, made to pull on, without fastenings, cut down at the sides, or lacing over the instep. Later, by the 1840s, *elastic-sided boots* were worn. The toes were rounded at the beginning of the century and became squared in the 1830s. In the 1840s glazed or patent leather was popular for boots and shoes and also for the toe-cap of boots of cloth or soft, light leathers, "boots, chamois, tipped black" (*Lady's Newspaper*, 1847).

At the beginning of the century very young boys might wear a *hat* with a high, stiff crown and narrow brim in straw or beaver, or a softer, lower-crowned, wider-brimmed style. So boys might wear some version of the top hat through childhood to manhood. For young boys a *peaked cap* with a low, flat crown became increasingly popular and by the 1820s had for them generally replaced the tall hat.

Younger boys in tunics, one wearing a peaked and tasselled hat; the older boy in a less usual style with jacket and trousers in one, with back opening. (J. Couts, *Practical Guide . . . c.* 1843.)

★ Beds. County Record Office.

PLATE 25

Two Eton boys, aged 12 and 13, in short tail coats. Both wear pantaloons, one has Hessian boots, the other socks and low shoes. He also has a seal dangling from a fob pocket. 1812.

Charles Augustus Ellis (Lord Howard de Walden) and his brother Augustus Frederick. H. Edridge. (Signed and dated.)
Reproduced by kind permission of Mr. L. G. Duke

PLATE 26

Harriet, aged 13, and her younger sister, in high-waisted frocks,
pelisses thrown open, shawls and round hats. 1818.

The Sisters Montagu. J. Ingres. (Signed and dated.) A. Montagu M.P.
Reproduced by kind permission of Mr. Victor Montagu

This peaked cap appeared in many forms, in cloth, holland, velvet or straw, with or without a tassel on the crown, "a cap of helmet form of Dunstable straw with black leather peak, and tassel" (*Lady's Newspaper*, 1847) and was the main style of hat for boys between the ages of 5 and 10 until the second half of the century. Schoolboys favoured the top hat. When Tom Brown went to Rugby, he "thought his cap a very knowing affair"—it was probably a peaked cap, for this was the 1830s—but neither this nor his hat, which was too shiny, suited the taste of his schoolfellow, so they went to Nixon's, the hatters, so that Tom could get "a regulation cat-skin at seven and sixpence".

Out of doors boys wore *overcoats* like those of adults, or cloaks, of cloth or woollen stuff. Tom Brown travelled to Rugby in "a Petersham coat with velvet collar, made tight after the abominable fashion of those days". The *Petersham coat* was a double-breasted frock-coat of the 1830s fitting in the upper half with full skirts and to the looser-coated 1850s appeared "an abominable fashion". Small boys in the 1840s often wore loose velvet coats and by the 1850s loose, straight overcoats were general.

During the 1820s the round jacket and skeleton suit were being replaced by the tunic:

> "the Jacket part of the Tunic or Frock is cut precisely in the same manner as the Skeleton Dress Jacket and the skirt of it upon the same principle as the Frock Coat skirt of adults".
>
> (*Tailor's Masterpiece*, c. 1830.)

This was worn up to about the age of 10.

> "In my opinion a boy when he leaves off wearing a tunic should only wear a single-breasted jacket. As he grows older, say at twelve years of age . . . a smartly made and well-fitted double-breasted jacket makes a nice kind of transition between the juvenile single-breasted jacket and the more manly frock."
>
> (Couts, *Practical Guide . . . c.* 1843.)

The *tunics* often had a broad belt at the waist and some kept the decoration of three rows of buttons on the front. They were made

C.C.E.–M

Younger boy in short jacket and peaked cap; older
boy in frock coat and tall hat. (J. Couts, *Practical Guide* . . .
c. 1843.)

in cloth, blue, brown and dark green being the usual colours, in
checkered wool, or in nankeen or jean.

The short round jacket did not completely disappear; the hussar
form was preserved throughout the nineteenth century in the dress
of boys at school, and made in black cloth became known as the
Eton jacket. At Eton black jackets replaced the usual coloured ones
when the school went into mourning for George III and then remained in wear, following the general tendency of men's fashions in
the 1820s, when black coats were appearing more and more and
coloured ones, except dark blue, less. Taine, writing his *Notes in
England* in the 1860s remarked on the boys at Harrow that the small
ones were in black jackets, the older ones in swallow-tail coats. This
style of jacket, usually with deep lapels was not only preserved at
Eton and Harrow, but was adopted as a school uniform and was
much worn by boys of school age to the end of the century. The

form cut straight at the back was preserved at Eton; other schools wore the pointed back (*West End Gazette*, 1889). The short jacket with ornamental buttons survived in some civilian uniforms, and, worn by page boys, can still sometimes be seen today.

The tunic dress was a youthful version of the frock-coat and its jacket was fitted and lined. But for school and everyday wear the younger boys, of about 5 to 7 wore loose tunics or overalls, with a broad belt holding the fullness at the waist. This form also was made in cloth or checkered woollen material or the strong cotton materials, and the trousers were matching or contrasting. Boys also wore pinafores with long sleeves, open behind. In *The Workwoman's Guide*, 1838, there are directions for making "Pinafores for boys of strong, black, glazed calico", with which they "often wear a band of patent leather". This loose garment was often called a *blouse*.

The loose tunics were, in form, not unlike the smocks worn by country boys, miniatures of those worn by farm labourers. These were usually made of linen, or cotton twill, natural-coloured, brown, or blue; they were full and loose, the fullness being gathered and stitched in a small panel, back and front, below the neck opening. Sometimes the decorative biasing of gathers, found on these *smock frocks* was used for pinafores of "gentlemen's children", but the smock-frock itself was a distinctive garment of the country boy. William Cobbett, in *Rural Rides* (1823) sees a boy at Billinghurst (Sussex):

> "Just such a chap as I was at his age and dressed in just the same sort of way, his main garment being a blue smock-frock, faded from wear and mended with pieces of new stuff, not yet faded."

During the 1840s and 1850s the skirt of the tunic dress grew shorter, becoming little more than a basque to the jacket, but the loose tunic remained long and belted and was the usual garment for young boys. It was by this time often made of velvet but checkered woollen materials were still popular, "one of those dark chequered woollen fabrics, now in general use for children's clothing" (*Lady's Newspaper*, 1849). Smaller boys, between the ages of 3 and 6 might wear these tunics, without trousers, with fancy stockings, and for out-of-door wear, often with gaiters of cloth or cashmere. Beneath the hem of the tunic the embroidered frills of short cambric trousers might be visible. The term "trousers", used for these short white ones, as well as the ankle-length trousers of stouter materials, was, during the 1850s, replaced by the word "drawers" for the frilled white ones as they gradually disappeared from sight and became underwear. Long trousers which at the beginning of the century were normal for boys of 2 upwards had now become the prerogative of those over 6. By the 1860s the age for wearing them had been raised to 9 or 10.

To bridge this period of transition from the frock, still worn to about the age of 3 or 4, boys might wear, as an alternative to the tunic a jacket and waistcoat over a pleated skirt, or over a frock with a pleated skirt. A boy's dress, for which a pattern was given in the *Englishwoman's Domestic Magazine*, 1857–8, was a jacket and waistcoat of velvet, trimmed with braid, with a skirt of Orleans cloth, completed by white drawers with broderie anglaise edging. The pleated skirts of these dresses and the frequent use of checkered materials made a costume which suggested Highland dress. The royal children wore a more definitely Highland style at Balmoral and were painted in Highland dress by Winterhalter in 1849:

Tunic in checkered wool, for a boy 5–7; with white muslin collar. (*Lady's Newspaper*, 1849.)

"The costume worn by the Prince of Wales, when at Balmoral, has set the fashion of adopting the complete Highland costume."

(*Lady's Newspaper*, 1852.)

Scotch suits were worn throughout the 1850s, 1860s and 1870s, but less generally by the 1880s:

"In boys' Scotch suits I saw several little dresses, the waistcoat and jacket of velvet, the kilt of tartan poplin, with scarf, brooch, sporran and Glengarry cap. If a cloth jacket is worn, woollen plaid is used for the kilt."

(*Englishwoman's Domestic Magazine*, 1867.)

The sartorial problem of the boy between the age of 3 and 7 was solved, more effectively, in the early 1860s, by the appearance of the *knickerbocker suit*. In 1863 the knickerbocker suit "reigns supreme" (*Englishwoman's Domestic Magazine*). Boys of 3 to 6 still wore the skirt with jacket and waistcoat, and these new suits at the age of 6 or 7: but by 1864, "little boys as soon as they leave off short frocks and pelisses, are clothed in jackets and knickerbockers" (*English-woman's Domestic Magazine*). The knickerbockers were short, full, closed and ending at the knee. They were worn with a short collar-less jacket, fastening at the neck only, which was like the fashionable short jacket of women's costume in the 1860s, the Zouave. The older boys wearing the knickerbocker suit also wore a waistcoat:

"Up to seven years the jacket is open over a full white shirt with frills; after that a waistcoat is worn. The trousers are full and wide and either straight or gathered at the knee. After the boy has out-grown white pique and brown holland nothing is more suitable for him than a suit of grey cloth or cashmere with no ornament but braid and gimp buttons of the same colour."

(*Englishwoman's Domestic Magazine*.)

Soon the age for wearing knickerbocker suits was extended, "Messrs Nicoll make these suits for boys of three to ten. They are made in serge, cloth, Melton and in drill, nankeen and other washing materials. They are very pretty and well made, the braiding being done by military braiders; the braiding on the ordinary suits is on the knees only in 'fern' 'pine' and 'coil' patterns; the braiding is chiefly in flat and Russian braid" (*Englishwoman's Domestic Magazine*, 1867). Braid was very much used in boys' suits at this time, for binding the edges and for these interlaced patterns, which appeared on knickerbocker suits. The knickerbockers were originally very full and closed at the knee, but by 1870 they were often in a more fitting, breeches-like style, and also in a style open at the knee. The fuller style disappeared by the 1880s, but the two other styles continued to be worn to the end of the century, "knickerbocker suits no longer have knickerbockers full. They are simply trousers cut off below the knee" (*Woman's World*, 1888). Drawers of flannel or cotton were worn beneath.

At the same time as the knickerbocker suit became popular the Navy was beginning to show an influence on boys' dress, which increased and lasted until the end of the century and beyond. Once again the Prince of Wales heralds the fashion. He was painted by Winterhalter in 1846 in the sailor dress which he had worn on board the *Victoria & Albert* that summer, but the earlier sailor dress did not follow the naval uniform so closely as this. During the 1860s a *sailor's blouse* with a square collar was worn with knickerbockers and a sailor hat, "a sailor hat in brown straw, trimmed with black ribbon with bow ends is suitable for little boys six to seven years of age" (*Englishwoman's Domestic Magazine*, 1861–2). During the 1860s and

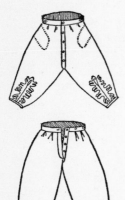

Knickerbockers for boy of 8. (*Cassell's Household Guide IV. c.* 1870.)

1870s this was a popular style of hat for boys whether they were wearing sailor dress or not. The sailor hat of these years was usually not the true sailor hat, but the yachting hat with low, flat crown and straight narrow brim. Sailor suits grew more and more popular especially after they were worn by the next generation of the royal family. "Sailor suits are always popular . . . and ever since the Prince of Wales's two sons have adopted the naval uniform the preference has increased" (*The Queen*, 1879). The suit was now seen in many forms. There was the man-o'-war suit, "correct as possible in all the details", complete with lanyard, knife and good conduct stripes. There were suits with knickerbockers, open or closed, and with long, bell-bottomed trousers; suits with blouses and suits with jackets:

"A boy before he rises to the dignity of trousers and jackets is never so happy as in a Middy suit or a Jack Tar; and these suits are now selling in thousands."

(*The Lady's World*, 1887.)

The middy suit had a jacket, the Jack Tar, a blouse. The hat was

Sailor suits. (*Weldon's Home Dressmaking*, 1897.)
Middy jacket and cap.

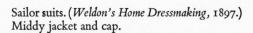

now the "Royal Tar hat"; a wide upcurving brim now replaced the narrow one of the 1860s and 1870s and the ribbon was often woven with the name of a ship; or a man-of-war cap, a round flat cap with a head band, also bearing the name of a ship, was worn. Originally a summer suit for seaside wear, the sailor suit was now worn throughout the year, in navy blue serge with cloth cap for winter, and for summer in white drill with straw hat:

> "This is a very sensible dress. The woollen underwear, the blue blouse for winter, the white one for summer, and blue serge trousers form a very good dress for a boy."
>
> (*Woman's World*, 1888.)

Slightly nautical too were the knitted jerseys which, worn at the seaside occasionally in the 1860s and 1870s had also become a popular fashion of the 1880s. They were worn especially by boys from about 3 to 7, Jersey costumes are better for boys than girls though equally comfortable for both:

Sailor suit for boy 4–10 years, 1897.
(*Weldon's Home Dressmaking.*)

"a robust agile rogue of six or seven never looks so well as when his shapely figure is displayed by his close-fitting knee breeches and jersey . . . being woollen they keep the body in a due state of warmth and prevent all chills . . . on the head is either a Tam-o-Shanter or a kind of brewer's cap . . . of the same kind of stockingnette as the suit".

(*Myra's Journal*, 1884.)

The tam-o'-shanter worn as a variant of the English man-of-war cap probably came from the French navy.

The most characteristic feature of the sailor dress was its blouse with open neck and vest in the opening and deep square collar. In the 1890s another style of blouse, sometimes called the *American blouse*, was worn with knickerbockers:

"a much more tidy garment than the formerly popular sailor blouse, which necessitates the addition of separate singlets, sailor collars, and then did not button up nicely to the neck".

(*Enquire Within, c.* 1895.)

Reefer coat for boy 12–16 years. 1897.
(*Weldon's Home Dressmaking*.)

Jersey and brewer's cap. (*Our Own Magazine*, 1886.)

This blouse had a centre front opening to button to the neck with a yoke-like, turn-down collar, usually frilled. It had a far less masculine look than the sailor blouse and was worn by both boys and girls. The collar repeated, with a difference, the frilled collars fashionable in the 1820s and 1830s. Another style which was in sharp contrast to the sailor and jersey suits was worn in the late 1880s and 1890s. This was the *Fauntleroy* suit, so-called because the hero of Mrs. Hodgson Burnett's book, *Little Lord Fauntleroy* (1886) wore one in black velvet. Velvet suits with lace collars were being worn as party dress a year or two before this. The *Tailor and Cutter* wrote in 1884, "many other fancy dresses are worn in the evening, especially those with much white lace and frilling on them", and in *The Lady* in 1885 there are illustrations and descriptions of this style, for "a little fellow of seven ... tunic and knickerbockers of sapphire blue velvet and sash of pale pink. Vandyke collar and cuffs, if not of old point lace, should be of Irish guipure". The use of velvet for boys' suits was nothing new; it had been a popular material since the 1840s, but the lace collar and sash, and even more, the long hair curling to the shoulders, which usually appeared with the costume, made it a distinctive type of dress,

> "We have little Cavaliers in plush tunics and knickerbockers with coloured silk sashes, Vandykes and collars."
>
> (*Woman's World*, 1888.)

There is no doubt that this was a fashion better loved by artistic and romantic mothers than by its wearers, "That confounded Little Lord Fauntleroy craze which led to my being given as a party dress the Little Lord Fauntleroy costume of black velvet and Vandyke collar was a curse. The other boys at the dancing class were all in white tops. Does this require explanation as a white top to one's sailor-suit instead of the blue of daily use or the pale blue of summer?" (1889.) (Compton Mackenzie (then 6 years old), *My Life and Times Octave One*, 1963.)

American blouse. (*Weldon's Home Dressmaking*, 1897.)

Older boys, those between the ages of 9 and 15 wore, during the 1860s, a short jacket, braided at the edges, fastening at the neck with a single button, with small, turn-down collar and no lapels or very short ones, with waistcoat and trousers, very like the jackets of younger boys, but generally less cut away. The short round jacket with deep lapels, the Eton jacket, worn with lighter trousers and waistcoat, was still worn as a school uniform and as a dress jacket.

By the late 1860s a jacket with three buttons, either with lapels or buttoning to the throat, like the lounge jacket which was beginning to be worn by men, was replacing the short, open jacket. For school or everyday wear, this with waistcoat and trousers was in tweed and "all of a piece". A blue or black cloth jacket, with white waistcoat and grey trousers was the smarter wear.

The tunic or blouse continued to be worn by young boys during the 1860s, often with a diagonal fastening from one shoulder and a belt with an S-buckle, but it was disappearing in the 1870s. It was replaced by a new form of blouse or belted jacket, the *Norfolk jacket*. In 1869 a boy's seaside dress was described as "a loose blouse

Norfolk suit. (*Weldon's Home Dressmaking*, 1897.)

or Norfolk shirt". Men also wore Norfolk "shirts" with pleats down the front, for country wear, and from this time boys also wore not only a loose belted jacket in this style, but a more fitted style, belted, with or without the pleating. This type of jacket replaced the short open jacket for younger boys during the 1870s and continued to be worn until the end of the century.

Another jacket, the *reefer jacket*, appeared in the 1860s, first as an overcoat:

> "Reefing jackets are worn as overcoats—I cannot say greatcoats— by mamma's little men."
>
> (*Englishwoman's Domestic Magazine*, 1867.)

This style which was double-breasted with three or four pairs of buttons and lapels was worn as a jacket with knickerbockers by younger boys in the 1870s, and remained popular to the end of the century. From the 1880s these jackets often appeared as part of the sailor suit. All jackets of the 1870s, lounge, Norfolk and reefer were

Boy's "Park" suit; Youth's tweed suit; Boy's "Sultan" suit. (Advertisement, *Jubilee Life of Queen Victoria*, 1887.)

worn longer than the jackets of the 1860s. Flannel jackets with patch pockets, known as *blazers* were worn for cricket and other sports and from this use became part of schoolboy dress:

> "the striped flannel jackets, under the familiar name 'blazer', brilliant in colouring, created for the river and the cricket field are worn on nearly all occasions now by girls and boys".
>
> (*The Lady's World*, 1887.)

Waistcoats were generally worn by older boys, usually of the same material as the jacket and trousers or knickerbockers; white waistcoats of cotton dimity or marcella were worn for full dress. Boys' waistcoats do not seem to have shared the decorative fabrics still used by men throughout the middle period of the century. The waistcoats buttoned up with a high V-shaped neck line with or without lapels, except in the dress waistcoats which were cut lower. Underwaistcoats of flannel were sometimes worn in winter.

The shirt had a pleated front panel and for smaller boys there was often a tab with buttonhole at the base of this so that the shirt could be buttoned to the drawers. The turn-down collar had become narrow by the 1860s and the wide, loosely-knotted bow or handkerchief of the 1850s had also grown narrower until it became the *shoe-string* tie of the 1860s. The Eton collar which was a deeper

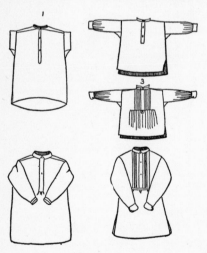

Flannel vest and nightshirt for a boy of 10 (left); Night shirt and day shirt for a boy of 8; boy's shirt (right). (*Cassell's Household Guide III & IV. c.* 1870.)

style was also worn in the 1860s and from this time until the end of the century was very generally worn, stiffly starched, by schoolboys. The *Tailor and Cutter* in 1884 recorded the habit of Eton boys wearing their collars inside the jacket, Harrow boys outside, and both styles were followed. Narrow stiff collars, standing or turned down were also worn during the last quarter of the century. The "sailor" tie, knotted with long ends and bow ties larger than the bows of the 1860s and early 1870s were both worn during this period.

In the 1860s *stockings* were often brightly coloured for boys wearing knickerbockers, in plaid to match the Scotch suits or striped in red or blue and white, or speckled,

> "Children's stockings in chiné pattern, ribbed, will be the favourite style for juvenile wear during the spring and summer, of stone and white with very little orange introduced are the newest style."
>
> (*The Queen*, 1865.)

As soon as trousers were worn socks replaced stockings,

> "The hose are of coloured worsted in the winter, generally of cotton in the summer. For dress occasions white are sometimes worn especially by little boys and may be of cotton, thread or silk. With a black velvet or velveteen suit black stockings are worn and for best it is handsome to choose these of silk. It is best taste to chose hose to match the colour of the suit, or dark brown or grey. Some certainly prefer scarlet; they are warmer and wash admirably."
>
> (*Cassell's Household Guide*, c. 1870.)

Striped stockings were still worn in the 1870s but had disappeared in the 1880s when dark stockings, black, brown or grey, replaced the lighter mixtures and white which had been worn earlier. Ribbed stockings were also popular in the 1880s, and wool was far more often worn than cotton,

> "Ribbed cashmere stockings for children have almost superseded those of cotton."
>
> (*The Lady's World*, 1887.)

Socks were then worn by boys below the age of 6.

During the 1850s and 1860s, short *boots* were generally worn, buttoning at the side, lacing at the front, or with elastic sides. Boots with front lacing were most popular in the 1860s and by 1864 a new style of boot was worn by boys and girls and women, with front lacing, shaped high in front and often finished with a tassel there:

> "Little boys and girls both wear the high boots, vandyked at the top, trimmed with cord and tassels, or else a small gaiter of cloth or cashmere, fastened with buttons over half-boots."
>
> (*Englishwoman's Domestic Magazine*, 1865.)

These boots were sometimes known as *Polish boots*:

> "Polish boots for boys' knickerbocker dress as well as ladies' walking dress."
>
> (*The Queen*, 1864.)

A less fashionable boot which began to appear at this time had pairs of metal hooks at the top instead of holes to finish off the lacing. Shoes were worn only by the very young, or by older boys for party wear. Boots were fairly high in the 1870s and 1880s and side buttoning was again popular in the 1880s. By the late 1880s also shoes were being worn again, with front lacing, or sometimes, for smaller boys, side buttoning.

The *peaked cap* was still worn in the 1860s, but with less variety of shape than it had in the first half of the century; it now usually had a flat round crown of cloth and a peak of patent leather; it was little worn after the 1860s. Up to the age of 7, "the round toque or Russian cap with the brim turned up and trimmed with a wide velvet ribbon to match the dress" (*Englishwoman's Domestic Magazine*, 1864) might be worn. For older boys a new style of hat with a low, rounded crown and a narrow, turn-up brim, in straw or hard felt, trimmed with a ribbon band, a low-crowned "*bowler*", joined the sailor hats and Scotch caps in the 1860s and continued to be worn until the end of the century.

> "And there's Freddy, looking more of a little man than ever . . . in an ulster coat and a round hat like Uncle William's."
>
> (*The Little Cousins* by Brenda, *c.* 1880.)

The cousins went to the Zoo where Laura's hat was stolen by a monkey. She was distressed not so much at the loss of her hat but

PLATE 27

Boy, aged 3, in frock and matching trousers. 1822.

Joseph Ginman Barratt. J. Hammond Jones (Signed and dated.)
Victoria and Albert Museum. Crown Copyright

PLATE 28

Boy and girls on left in short low-necked frocks, socks and ankle-strap slippers. Boy (the future King Edward VII) wearing a suit in the style of a "middy". The girl on the right (Princess Royal) with drawers showing below her full skirt. c. 1847.

"The Royal Family in the Nursery" Victoria and Albert Museum. Crown Copyright

because "I shall feel so ashamed going through the streets without a hat". So the gallant Freddy gave her his round felt hat, which fitted her well and turned up the hood of his ulster to cover his own head. Top hats were worn by older boys for formal occasions. The close-fitting cloth cap, with peak, which had been worn as a cricketing cap came into more general use at the end of the century.

Ulsters, overcoats with belt or half-belt across the back and often with a hood or cape were worn from the 1870s to the end of the century:

> "For two years now, the youngsters have taken almost unanimous possession of the ulster and almost everywhere are there seen wee little men from four years old and upwards dressed in the ulster."
>
> (*Tailor and Cutter*, 1875.)

(*a*) Girl in fur tippet and her own hat. (*b*) Boy in ulster and bowler hat. (*c*) Boy in jacket, knickerbockers and bowler. (*d*) Girl wearing the boy's bowler. (*e*) Boy with ulster hood turned up. 1880. (*Little Cousins* by Brenda.)

They were usually cut very long. *Inverness capes*, loose coats with a deep cape were worn from the 1860s, "Boys wearing out of doors Inverness capes and paletots, the latter frequently in grey cloth" (*Englishwoman's Domestic Magazine*, 1863). *Paletot* was a general term for overcoat. The Chesterfield, a straight coat without a waist seam, with fly fastening was worn by boys as well as men from the 1860s, sometimes with a velvet collar and in the 1880s sometimes with an added cape. The double-breasted reefer coat, in rough cloth, worn rather short, was a popular overcoat of the 1860s and continued to be worn in the 1870s and 1880s when it was usually longer.

.   .   .

Girls' clothes 1800–c. 1840; underwear, footwear 1800–1900

Susan Sibbald, writing many years later, recalled her much-loved niece, Margaret, at the age of 5, in about 1806, "I think I can see her now in a white muslin frock and red morocco shoes which children then wore." This serves well for a picture of almost any small girl of that time, in a white *muslin dress*, with coloured shoes and sash. These dresses of white muslin were not very different, except in size, from those which they had worn as babies and which they would wear until they became young women at about the age of 16. Elizabeth Grant, who was born in 1797, remembered the dresses she and her sisters had worn up to about 1813:

> "My sisters and I had hitherto been all dressed alike. In summer we wore pink gingham or nankeen frocks in the morning, white in the afternoon. Our common bonnets were of coarse straw lined with green and we had tippets to all our frocks. The best bonnets were of finer straw lined with white and we had silk spencers of any colour that suited my mother's eye. In winter we wore dark stuff frocks, black and red for a while—the intended mourning for the king. At night always scarlet stuff with bodices of black velvet and bands of the same at the hem of the petticoat. While in England our wraps were of the pelisse form and made of cloth; the bonnets did in the Highlands, but on outgrowing the pelisses they were replaced by cloaks with hoods made of tartan."
>
> (*Memoirs of a Highland Lady* 1797–1827, 1950.)

Always high-waisted for the first twenty years of the century, the *dresses* for morning wear were usually printed cotton, spotted checked or with small sprigged patterns, or the stronger, natural-coloured nankeen. For best wear, white muslin, with work or narrow insertions of lace on the bodice front, sleeves and hem, was generally worn, although, particularly after about 1815, best dresses were often made in silk, in pale colours. "Stuff" frocks, that is of some light woollen fabric, were worn in winter. Low necks and short sleeves were general—hence the need for tippets—although some dresses for morning wear had high necks and long sleeves. Dresses fastened at the back with drawstrings at the neck and waist, but some had the back open to the hem, fastening with buttons. For younger girls buttonholes were placed each side of the back opening at the waist to fasten on to a button on the stays to keep the dress in place. Shoes and sash brought colour to the white muslin dress. The sash, tied in a bow at the back, was a very important part of a girl's dress. When they discovered that their cousin, Fanny Price, had only two sashes, the fashionable Misses Bertram, "could not but hold her cheap" (*Mansfield Park*, 1811–13).

During the 1820s girls' dresses, like those of their mothers, grew longer in the bodice and fuller in the skirt and sleeve. With frills at the hem, coloured embroidery and ribbon trimmings, they were losing the simplicity which had marked them since the 1780s. But white muslin with a coloured sash, in changing shapes, remained for a long time almost a uniform for a young girl's party wear. The coloured shoes worn at the beginning of the century were gradually replaced by black ones, and by the end of the 1820s, square-toed, *sandal shoes*, with ribbons crossing over the ankles were very generally worn, although a high-fronted style, with ties was still worn for walking.

Short jackets—*spencers*—or short capes—*tippets*—were worn over the dresses out of doors. These often matched the print or nankeen dresses, but coloured silk ones were usually worn with white muslin. For winter there were cloth pelisses—long coats. Georgiana Sitwell, who was born in 1824, remembering the clothes of her childhood, wrote:

"one winter we were all dressed like a row of gentianellae, in dark Prussian blue cloth pelisses, with tippets and cuffs trimmed with grey rabbit fur, and black beaver bonnets".

(*Two Generations*, O. Sitwell, 1940.)

Hats or bonnets were generally of beaver in winter and straw in summer, although soft bonnets of cloth, print, nankeen or silk were worn, especially by children up to 5 years of age. At the beginning of the century a low-crowned, wide-brimmed straw hat, tied under the chin with ribbon was worn, and although straight-brimmed bonnets and then bonnets of other shapes, following the sequence of women's fashions, replaced this style, it remained for country and informal wear until the 1850s. Georgiana Sitwell remembered also, "when we were a little older . . . the size of the bonnets and of the gigot sleeves was overwhelming, but the former were useful as parasols were not used". They often wore straw bonnets trimmed with green silk ribbon, a favourite combination for children and country wear. The sad cry of a girl for a new bonnet and spencer has survived in a letter of Betty Bury, who was born in 1800, to her elder sister Mary, probably about 1815:

Girl in pelisse with tippet; cap under high-crowned bonnet. (A. B. Love, s. and d. 1828. Victoria and Albert Museum.)

"the reason is why I write because i want a few things my Bonnet
is so dirty I can scarcely for shame wear it. I wish you would send me
another for if I get this cleaned I have no other to wear while it is
cleaned and besides my new one would fit me all next summer for
if I stop here (with her aunt in Manchester) I must have things it is
getting quite cold it is time to begin to wear Spensers and my
Nankeen one is very shabby I wish you would send me one and a
Bonnet. I hope my Father told you about my Green Frock it is
quite rotten. I wish you would send me some stuff for a new one."
(Letter preserved in Gallery of English Costume, Manchester.)

Girls still wore caps beneath the bonnet but after the first few years
of the century, did not generally wear them otherwise in the daytime. They might still wear caps in bed at night until the middle of
the century.

The most characteristic feature of the dress of girls during the first
thirty years of the century was their wearing, and after a while,
showing, *trousers* of white cambric which reached to the ankles.
These trousers seem to have been very generally worn in place of
petticoats from the first years of the century, but at that time girls,
even small ones, still wore long dresses to the ankles and it was not
until the 1820s that the dresses shortened enough to make the trousers
visible enough to seem part of the dress for girls well out of babyhood. As one would expect this style was a matter of differing
opinions amongst parents and a point of sartorial conflict between
generations, though, at this time, the younger generation may not
generally have had the freedom of expression allowed to the Princess
Charlotte in her conversation with Lady de Clifford (*Glenbervie
Journals*, 1910):

"She was sitting with her legs stretched out after dinner and showed
her drawers which it seems she and most young women now wear.
Lady de Clifford said, 'My dear Princess Charlotte, you shew your
drawers—I never do but when I can put myself at ease—Yes, my
dear, when you get in and out of a carriage—I don't care if I do—
Your drawers are too long—I do not think so, the Duchess of Bedford's are much longer and they are bordered with Brussels lace.'"

This was in 1811 when the Princess was 15 years old. Drawers at this time were not in general wear as an undergarment by English-women, but they were worn by girls, though it was mainly girls younger than the Princess who showed any length of them, and it was particularly in the 1820s when it became general for the frocks of younger girls to end between the knee and the ankle and show the trousers which reached the ankle. *Leglets,* for the lower part of the legs only were also worn, either attached to shorter drawers at the knee, or covering the legs of trousers, fastened on to them by buttons and loops, to keep the trouser legs clean. In the late 1820s another style appeared, "Turkish trousers" with the legs full and gathered into a frilled band at the ankle. The trousers were trimmed with narrow openwork edgings or frills and puffs of muslin. Words-worth's sister-in-law, Sara Hutchinson, wrote of the practice with disapproval in 1824:

> "I am sorry to hear that little dear Good-Good (Mary Hutchinson, born 1817) has been breeched—for some of the faculty opine that it is much better that females should not—and Mary H. gave up the practice of putting her Girls into Trowsers from her own experience that it was injurious."
>
> (Letters of Sara Hutchinson, 1800–35, 1954.)

But this juvenile fashion, like so many others, grew up with its wearers, and by 1838, *The Workwoman's Guide* could state that trousers or drawers are worn by men, women and children of all classes and almost all ages, under different names of trousers and drawers. Generally the term drawers was used for the undergarment, and trousers for the visible leggings. Girls' trousers generally buttoned on to their stays but some were made with their own bodice.

As the skirts widened in the 1830s trousers were no longer a substitute for petticoats. Flannel *petticoats* were made either to fasten on to the stay bodice or as a single garment and upper petticoats of cambric were also worn, usually on a bodice. Long narrow trousers were at first still worn beneath the widening skirts, but during the 1840s they grew shorter and wider, so that by the middle of the century they appeared as little more than embroidered frills visible beneath the hem of the dress at whatever level it happened to be.

This varied according to the age of the child. A girl of 4 or 5 by 1850 wore frocks to just below the knee, and these lengthened as she grew older, so that a girl of 8 or 9 had a dress just short of the ankle with the white frills showing beneath.

With the lengthening bodice of the 1840s the corded bodice which had been worn as *stays* was replaced as girls grew into their teens by a more rigid garment, designed to train the figure into fashionable lines:

> "Alice has been afflicted with a pair of stays with bones which cause infinite trouble and dismay to the whole household. However she has a gown made upon them which would astonish you. It is Douglas plaid—tight waist, tight sleeves, and a most wax-like fit and when she appears in the said gown she looks most awfully tall."
>
> (*Cecilia*, Life and Letters of Cecilia Ridley, 1819–45.)

This was in 1840 and Alice was 11 years old.

The daughters of fashionable mothers were the chief sufferers. There was a strong current of opinion against the early wearing of boned stays "for the girl stays and corsets of all kinds must be forbidden during the whole period of childhood" (*Dictionary of Daily Wants*, 1861), and the lighter type of corded stays continued to be used, by those less devoted to the early display of the fashionable figure in their daughters.

Little girl in embroidered muslin frock with twin flounces, worked petticoat appears below. 1852. (*The World of Fashion*, September.)

Girls started to wear a *chemise* which was of the current fashion between the age of 5 and 8, but kept their own style of drawers to the end of the century until they were 9 or 10. These had side openings, instead of the open-legged style worn by women. As their small skirts spread out, in imitation of larger skirts, in the 1840s and 1850s, their petticoats grew fuller; and more starched and frilled to support the skirts. In the 1860s little girls, if fashionable, had their own small crinoline frames. In 1863 the *Englishwoman's Domestic Magazine* referred to knitted petticoats which were worn "beneath their tiny cages", but two years later to "girls of five or six wearing with their evening frocks two or three muslin skirts underneath in place of the crinoline".

In the late 1870s and 1880s, the "union" or *combination* garment, which was chemise and drawers combined appeared:

"The combination garment . . . forms a complete and most sanitary costume, and were it not for the sake of appearances is all that is needed for summer wear; but other clothing is required in winter

Different types of chemises for a girl of 8.
(*Cassell's Household Guide II. c.* 1870.)

for warmth and in summer for the sake of that tyrant appearance."

(A. S. Ballin, *Science of Dress,* 1885.)

Night and day *vests* of flannel had been recommended in 1838, particularly for delicate children and during the second half of the century there was a growing advocacy of the wearing of woollen undergarments:

> "flannel should be worn next to the skin during the day and put off at night. In summer cotton may be substituted and flannel resumed in the autumn. If flannel should prove irritation to the skin fine fleecy hosiery will be easily endured and will greatly conduce to the preservation of health." (*Dictionary of Daily Wants,* 1861.)

The object of the garment was to lessen the pressure and weight of clothing at the waist, but combinations never completely superseded the chemise and drawers although they were very generally adopted during the last twenty years of the century:

> "It must have been just as I was in my teens that we both started wearing merino underclothes. Up to then we had linen, not cotton, chemises and drawers."
>
> (Louisa K. Haldane, born 1863, *Friends and Kindred,* 1911.)

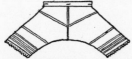

Nightdress and drawers for a girl of 8. (*Cassell's Household Guide II. c.* 1870.)

In *Goodbye for the Present*, Eleanor Acland recollected vividly in 1935, the discomfort which accumulated in a child's underwear at this time and the complication of buttoning at the waist:

"What I, on behalf of my fifty-years ago self most envy the little girls of today is the fewness and simplicity of their garments. . . . We, too, put on first of all a vest. Then a chemise, a garment, whose use was never apparent to us, but we were given to understand that it wouldn't be at all 'nice' to go without it. It was made of calico and reached to the knees. Next 'stays' a strip of wadded pique whose use was unmistakable. In addition to the five buttons that fastened our stays up the back, they had a number of other buttons at various levels and intervals round the waist. Two of these held up the elastic 'spenders' of our stockings; the five buttonholes of our drawers belonged to the other three, and yet two more were buttoned into two holes in the band of our flannel petticoat. Over that came a white petticoat made with a bodice. The edges of all the white garments were decorated with rather scratchy cambric trimming. . . . I have forgotten the stockings themselves, long black stockings reaching above the knee, woollen in winter, thick cotton in summer."

Little girls in night gowns. 1892. (From *A Soldier's Children* by John Strange Winter.)

This child had the worst of both worlds, the vest (? of wool) was probably added in accordance with the "wool next to the skin" ideas, but the traditional cotton chemise was not discarded.

White cotton *stockings* were the general wear until the second half of the century. Sometimes these had openwork patterns in the lower part over the ankle. Occasionally there were silk stockings for party wear. In the 1860s striped stockings in red, blue or magenta were sometimes worn for everyday, mainly by the younger children. In the 1870s cotton began to give place to wool and black and brown stockings to replace white ones, for girls and boys alike. Stockings got a little longer, over the knee, and there was always difficulty in keeping them up.

> "How to keep up the stockings really seems one of the questions of the day—wide silk elastic band, over the knee, not under. The French fashion of light cloth gaiters is a most sensible and wise one . . . yet of all French fashions this has been least adopted in England."
>
> (*The Queen*, 1879.)

The age of wearing socks was now extended to about 6 or 7,

> "Socks are now fashionable for children of seven years and younger."
>
> (*Ladies' Treasury*, 1881.)

By the 1830s the sandal shoe with ribbons crossing over the instep was the usual style for best wear; for everyday and outdoor wear short boots, just covering the ankle, in kid or cashmere, with leather toe caps, with side-buttoning or lacing and then with elastic sides, were worn by girls of all ages from 2 upwards. Shoes of the 1830s and 1840s had a small bow at the centre front, which by the 1860s grew into a rosette; at this time too some of the shoes were ornamented like women's shoes with a cut-out pattern over silk on the toe. During the late 1860s the front-buttoning boot with a tassel at the top was worn by girls as well as boys, and from this time low heels appeared on their boots and shoes. Long, buttoned boots continued to be worn in the 1870s and 1880s, a source of affliction to their wearers:

"The worst worry in going out was my boots, which came far above the ankle with endless buttons that needed a button hook to do them up."

(*London Child of the Seventies*, M. V. Hughes, 1934.)

Shoes which buttoned or laced over the instep were also worn from the 1880s and were more general in the 1890s, although the buttoned and laced boots were still worn. A shoe with a bar over the instep also appeared in the 1890s and for party wear older girls wore a low-fronted shoe with a small buckle. Ankle-strap shoes were worn throughout the century by very young girls only.

Girls' clothes c. 1840–1870

In *dresses* the proportion of bodice and skirt which had been changing gradually during the 1820s and 1830s, were, by the 1840s, completely reversed, when the bodice of a small girl's dress was generally longer than its skirt. The skirt which ended at the knee for girls of 4 or 5 was full and had its fullness increased by flounces, which appeared on many dresses between 1840 and 1870.

"a favourite style is a silk dress, the skirt almost covered with pinked flounces, the corsage made low and worn with a muslin chemisette."

(*Lady's Newspaper*, 1850.)

White muslin, with coloured ribbon sash also continued to be worn for party dresses.

Small girls, like their baby sisters and brothers continued to wear very low dresses and short sleeves. By the 1850s Mrs. Merrifield, in *Dress as a Fine Art* (1854) could say "It is fortunate for the present generation that it is the fashion for the dresses of even little girls to be made as high as the throat": but she complains of the low necks and short sleeves which still appeared in what was called full dress, "Girls are suffered to shiver at Christmas in muslin dresses with bare necks and arms, in which the dress to stay up at all had to be tight at the waist and even so kept slipping off the wearer's shoulders." She quoted Dr. J. F. South's *Domestic Surgery*, "If then you wish your children, girls especially, to have the best of health and a good constitution let them wear flannel next their skin and woollen stockings in winter; have your girls' chests covered to the collar bone and their shoulders in, not out of their dresses." The evidence of surviving photographs does suggest that not all children suffered from these low necks all the time, although when low bodices were worn they were usually very low indeed, leaving the shoulders quite exposed. Many of the day dresses had their own *matching jackets* or capes and a muslin jacket over a silk dress or a silk jacket over a muslin dress was a favourite style for best summer dress. For winter the dress might be of merino or cashmere, with a velvet jacket:

> "for very little girls, crimson is a favourite colour for cashmere dresses and the pardessus for children from five to seven years old may be made either of black or coloured velvet".
>
> (*Lady's Newspaper*, 1850.)

Printed cottons with small sprigged patterns which were no longer fashionable in adult wear were still used for children's dresses in the 1840s and 1850s. There was also an increased use of silk, which had previously not been regarded as suitable for children, except for party wear. According to the *Lady's Newspaper* in 1851, silk was suitable for the ages 5 to 7, with pinked flounces as its usual form of trimming. Poplin was thought a very suitable material during the 1850s and 1860s, and alpaca was also used in the 1860s. White piqué which was used for jackets in the 1850s became a favourite fabric for dresses in the 1860s and 1870s, replacing the lighter muslin for everyday wear, a change which was lamented by one writer in 1873, "the former (muslin dresses) being smarter, and certainly softer and prettier in material than the white piqué now in vogue". Piqué, however, had many advantages and dresses of piqué with braided trimming were very popular between 1860 and 1875, "For children of all ages, there are delightful little piqué costumes and pelisses, the only trimming of which is a raised embroidery worked on the piqué which washes perfectly and requires simply starching and ironing." Braiding which had been used as a trimming on children's garments from the 1820s was particularly popular during the 1860s. But dresses of plaid or tartan pattern, in poplin, silk or wool, were perhaps the most general fashion of all between 1840 and 1870.

Events in Italy gave little girls a new form of dress in the early 1860s. This was the *Garibaldi costume*, which was originally a bright red blouse worn with a white skirt, but variants of this appeared,

(a)   (b)

(c)   (d)

(a) Grey cloth paletot with pagoda sleeves and epaulettes. 1862.
(b) Short loose paletot edged to match the skirt. Velvet hat, Tasselled boots, 1866.

(c) Silk dress trimmed with plaid silk. Swiss belt. 1864.
(d) Dress of grey Mousseline de soie spotted with cerise. Chemisette. Swiss belt. 1864.

(a), (b), and (d) wear hair nets.   (*The World of Fashion*.)

making a general fashion of a separate skirt and blouse, or chemisette, as a blouse was often called at this time. Women wore a blouse and skirt only as very informal dress, in the mornings, at home, so that at this time it was mainly a girl's fashion.

Otherwise the dress of girls in the 1860s was very much a miniature of their mothers'. What this might mean can be seen in Charlotte Yonge's picture of a 9-year-old girl, the somewhat over-dressed Ida, of *The Stokesley Secret* (1861):

> "Her hat was of black chip, edged and tied with rose-coloured ribbon, and adorned with a real bird, with glass eyes, black plumage, except the red crest and wings. She wore a neatly-fitting little fringed black polka, beneath which spread out in fan-like folds her flounced pink muslin, coming a little below her knees, and showing her worked drawers, which soon gave place to her neat stockings and dainty little boots. She held a small white parasol, bordered with

Top: For girl of 8, summer dress, silk with muslin tunic and dress in two colours, braid and bead trimming. Below: Tunic dress for girl of 8 to 10. Plain dress for girl of 8. (*Cassell's Household Guide. II. c.* 1870.)

pink and deeply fringed, over her head, and held a gold-clasped Prayer-book in her hand."

The *polka* was a short jacket with open sleeves usually shaped to the waist. In the 1860s jackets or coats, which were usually half to three-quarter length, were often called paletots, like those of boys. The sleeve changed to a wide shaped form, closed at the wrist, the same shaping as the sleeves of women's dresses and coats. They were generally rather plain, made of silk, velvet or wool, including the heavier cloths. If there was trimming it was usually of velvet bands or braiding. *Cloaks* were worn throughout the middle period of the century and in the 1860s they were sometimes of scarlet wool, "little girls in scarlet, gipsy cloaks" (*Englishwoman's Domestic Magazine*).

Girls of the 1850s wore miniatures of the fashionable *bonnet*, in beaver or drawn, i.e. gathered, silk, trimmed with a single feather waving across them, or with ribbon, but they also wore hats, with rather flat crowns and wide brims for everyday wear, particularly in the country,

Outdoor dress; velvet paletot and silk bonnet.
(*World of Fashion*, 1852.)

PLATE 29

Boy in tunic with drawers showing below; socks and laced
boots. Girl in low-necked flounced dress with drawers showing, socks and buttoned boots. 1856.

*A. H. Fox. Reproduced by permission of the Committee,
the Christchurch Mansion Museum*

PLATE 30

Fashionable girl on left in blouse, skirt and jacket, wearing a smart hat and buttoned boots. Poor girl, with baby, in plain dress, pinafore and laced boots. 1870.

"The Park Bench." F. P. Shuckard

Reproduced by kind permission of M. Newman Ltd., 43a Duke Street, London

"round straw hats whether Leghorn or sewed straw are always a requisition for the country, especially trimmed with broad ribbon, fringed at the ends".

(Lady's Newspaper, 1851.)

Later in the 1850s, similar hats were worn by women, but for them it was a style strictly limited to country and seaside wear:

"straw hats which in large towns are only worn by children or very young girls will be universally worn in the country or at the seaside".

(Englishwoman's Domestic Magazine, 1861–2.)

The hair was usually parted in the middle and smooth over the head, falling in ringlets on the shoulders or braided in looped-up plaits. In the 1860s it was drawn back from the forehead, sometimes held with a band and then left loose or held in a net at the back, or plaited with the plaits, still gathered up, taken to the back of the head. By this time the bonnet had disappeared for girls' wear and small round or oval hats were general, both for small boys and girls of all ages. Once again girls were ahead of their mothers in wearing hats instead of bonnets. By 1863 a higher crown appeared, "somewhat in the shape of a cone" with a flat narrow brim, and by the late 1860s the narrow brim curved up at the sides. For summer the hats were usually straw bound and trimmed with coloured silk or velvet ribbon. For winter they were of velvet or felt, which appeared more often in children's hats than in women's hats at this time. Feathers

Velvet hat with feather; hair in net; velvet-trimmed cloth coat. (*Englishwoman's Domestic Magazine*, 1862.)

C.C.E.—O

were a general trimming for when a more elaborate hat was worn. During the 1870s the brims either grew wider, and by 1880 were turning up at one side or the back, or had disappeared altogether making a high-crowned toque. Fur hats were popular in this shape during the 1880s. Smaller girls again wore bonnets, soft-crowned, with the brim rising in a ruched peak.

Girls' clothes c. 1870–1900

Dresses of the 1870s had the double skirt which was a feature of women's fashions, tied up to give a similar bustle effect, and then, in the late 1870s, were made in princess form:

> "The princess form is that now usually made for young girls—that is there is no separate bodice, but both that and the skirt are in one and they are not tight-fitting."
>
> (*Ladies' Treasury*, 1876.)

That they were not tight-fitting was the concession to youth. These dresses showed the same fashionable combination of two materials, wool and silk, silk and velvet, and the same details of trimming, the pleated frills, and puffed plastrons as in grown-up styles:

> ". . . our bridesmaids dresses of white cashmere with red velvet panel on one side of the skirt and various red plastrons. We had muslin caps, like the maids' caps, with red bows and a spray of artificial heather."
>
> 1876. (*Friends and Kindred*, L. K. Haldane, 1961.)

The draped overdress fashionable in women's dress at this time also had its youthful versions:

> "When I was about nine years old (*c.* 1876), there came in a fashion to dress little girls like miniature Newhaven fishwives—striped cotton skirts, turned up tunics of blue serge, striped cotton collar and cuffs and little apron with pockets. What to our elders was just a pretty style was for us a passion—not to be like a Newhaven fishwife was a tragedy."
>
> (*Edinburgh's Child*, E. Sellars, 1961.)

A "fishwife" tunic was popular for several years after this:

"Fishwife tunics, turned up at the edge and draped very high at the back, and ornamented with a sash with long loops and ends, are also much worn by little girls, but the dresses for older girls, those who are over twelve, are chiefly made with plain pleated or gathered skirts, with or without a puff at the back and with very simple draperies, if any."

(Myra's Journal, 1885.)

The mixture of striped cotton and serge in these dresses, continued to the late 1880s:

"Some pretty canvas with a brocaded anchor, makes charming Fishwife dresses, which are repeated in serge with a striped skirt."

(Lady's World, 1887.)

Serge was becoming a popular material for girls' dresses by the end of the 1870s. It was regarded as specially suitable for seaside wear because children were less likely to catch cold from wet serge than wet cotton and it quickly spread into general use, for coats as well as dresses for boys and girls alike. The stronger cottons were also worn, particularly in striped patterns and in the 1880s a loosely woven canvas-like cotton, often embroidered appeared in many dresses. Holland dresses were braided in bright colours and both these and the cotton dresses were often trimmed with a good deal of white openwork embroidery, now bought in ready-made frills and insertions. Thin woollen materials were much used for best winter dresses, sometimes embroidered, especially for younger children, and thin silks were also being worn by the end of the 1880s.

In the early 1870s the loose *jackets* of the 1860s were still worn out of doors but generally in the short form only. For any longer jacket, a basqued form appeared, matching the line of the dress, and both the front and sleeves fitted more closely.

"For outdoor wear as a mantle, a little girl of eight years of age may wear a tight-fitting jacket; or one nearly tight, called a demi-adjuste, or a loose jacket. These may be made of cloth, trimmed velvet, lined red flannel for winter. For summer, they can be of black silk trimmed with silk passementerie, beads and fringe; or of muslin or they can be composed of any material corresponding with the dress of the little girl."

(*Cassell's Household Guide*, *c.* 1870.)

During the middle period of the century, 1840–80, black coats and jackets were regarded as suitable and normal wear for girls of all ages. It was also regarded as normal and even necessary for very small children to wear deep mourning:

> "My grandfather died when I was nine (*c.* 1878) and I was at once clothed in black cashmere, so lavishly trimmed about with crape that I must have looked like a miniature widow of that period, without the cap."

(*Edinburgh's Child.*)

The many small black dresses surviving now in museums suggest that this was a fairly general habit. To the end of the century children might still wear black for the deaths of very near relatives, but during the last quarter of the century it became more limited in range and intensity. The writer of *How to dress on a shilling a day* (*c.* 1875) reflects this change:

> "It is desirable that children should be put into mourning dress as seldom as possible."

Five year old girl in deep mourning for her mother. 1863. (From an original photograph.)

A strong belief in the protective virtues of red flannel gave little girls red flannel petticoats and jacket linings, but some mothers were more cautious than others about this. When Mrs. Haldane, at the age of about 14, had her first shop-made dress in the late 1870s, "a chocolate homespun dress and jacket" she was told not to forget to remind the shop that the jacket must be lined with red flannel, "although other girls when they took off their jackets did not exhibit red flannel linings" (*Friends and Kindred*, 1961).

A straight-fronted, rather tight-sleeved style of *coat*, cut with a basque, or long, with fullness at the back was worn in the late 1870s and early 1880s. A double-breasted style now appeared,

> "coats being double-breasted can defy the often mischievous results of rain and wind".
>
> (*Ladies' Treasury*, 1880.)

Waterproof coats were being worn from the early 1880s,

> "It is a great boon that woollen goods can be so perfectly water-proofed now without any rubber showing."
>
> (*Woman's World*, 1890.)

Waterproof cape. (*Housewife*, 1896.)

Fur capes were occasionally worn in the late 1860s and were popular by the late 1880s, "good fur tippets" were recommended then for girls when they were skating (*ibid., 1888*). Fur was also used as a trimming on coat collars and cuffs.

The Garibaldi blouse which had been worn in the 1860s was followed by the *sailor blouse* with a deep collar like those worn by boys in their sailor suits. These sailor suits which by 1880 had become almost a uniform for boys were being adapted for girls, who wore a sailor blouse with a pleated skirt in navy serge or white drill. This style, at first a seaside dress, was, by the 1880s, adopted as a general fashion.

> "Sailor costumes are very elaborate for girls this summer made principally in two colours; white and blue or navy blue and pale blue are the favourite combinations; some are entirely navy blue trimmed with silver or gold braid. These costumes are for walking purposes, to be worn in the park and they are totally different to the rougher costumes meant for seaside wear."
>
> (*Myra's Journal*, 1884.)

The more formal sailor dress usually comprised, with the pleated skirt, a double breasted reefer jacket, as described for the 1860s:

Seaside frock, white drill. (*Queen*, 1896.)

"For seaside wear, girls as well as boys, have discovered the comfort of the pea-jackets (the earlier name for a reefer jacket) with collar and gold buttons of the most nautical aspect."

(*The Lady's World,* 1887.)

This style brought the dress of girls a little farther away from the main stream of women's fashion and nearer to the dress of their brothers:

"Sisters follow their brothers' example as nearly as they can in sailor suits made with petticoats."

(Ibid.)

By the 1890s often made in other materials, tweeds and smooth cloths, this *jacket and skirt* had become almost a uniform for girls. Full-length coats, that is coats covering the dress, to just below the knee, which was now the general length up to the age of 14, were also made in this style.

With the sailor suits, sailor hats, low-crowned with wide turning-up brims were worn and remained popular to the end of the century. A stiff boater shape was also worn, and another popular style, for girls as well as boys, was the tam-o'-shanter, a cap with a soft, beret-like crown, often of crocheted or knitted wool. This was usually worn with a jersey.

For playing on the beach and in the water there were "the rougher costumes meant for seaside wear" which still sound bulky and elaborate for their purpose. A complete outfit for the seaside was described in *The Housewife* in 1896:

"Next to the skin the child is to wear a thin woollen gauze combination, very short in the leg; over that a stay body to which is buttoned a pair of blue serge knickerbockers unlined. Over that only one skirt is worn and that had seven flat buttons sewn on the wrong side near the hem. On the upper part of the skirt are seven corresponding loops so that for paddling the desired shortness is easily attained by buttoning the bottom of the dress to the loops. A little blouse of white serge or washing silk is worn with the skirt and a short blue serge jacket added according to the weather or time of day. . . . Long merino stockings should be worn, which should pass under the knickers. To take off the effect of the sun's rays on the head it is well to give the hat a complete green head lining, using a dull green so as to avoid arsenical dyes."

Children were wearing *bathing dresses* by the 1860s:

"About 1869 we went to stay . . . in Cannes. . . . That summer sea bathing had been prescribed for me (now about six years old). My red flannel nightgowns were made into bathing dresses!"
(*Friends and Kindred*, L. K. Haldane.)

A *bathing costume* for a little boy or girl in blue serge and white braid appeared in the *Englishwoman's Domestic Magazine* in 1870. In an article on children's dress of about the same date, a bathing dress for a girl is described, also made of serge, with short puffed sleeves and with trousers, "cut by any drawers the child wears, left unlined" (*Cassell's Household Guide*). Jersey material was used for a one-piece bathing dress from the 1880s, "It (jersey) has proved so popular that children's new bathing suits are combination garments of dark blue jersey material" (*The Lady's World*, 1887).

The wearing of the sailor suit and the jersey suit was bringing girls' dress nearer to the dress of boys, and according to *The Lady's World*, 1887, girls as well as boys were wearing, when on holiday by the sea, the "blazer" of rower and cricket-field over their jersey bodices:

"And the striped flannel jackets, under the familiar name of 'blazers' are worn on nearly all occasions now by girls and boys. The girls often have a jersey beneath which gives perfect freedom to the young limbs, even in the roughest exercise."

During the 1880s the influence of the practical wear of the nursery and the schoolroom was producing another style of dress which was to give girls their own distinctive fashion in the 1890s, diverging from women's dress. Pinafores to protect the dress, or worn instead of a dress in the nursery or schoolroom had been a part of children's dress from the beginning of the century. In the 1830s these pinafores, which were as completely enveloping as dresses, were usually made of holland, cut full from a high neck or yoke and belted. Such loose overalls never completely disappeared from use, but for girls a more decorative and less useful pinafore developed, so that there were pinafores and dress pinafores. The dress *pinafore* continued its decorative way to the end of the century, in white muslin with frills and insertions of lace and embroidery, while the other style, called in the 1870s a frock pinafore, which could be "worn all day in and out of doors without any frock" (*Cassell's Household Guide, c.* 1870) was beginning to influence the contemporary dress. By 1880s these pinafores were often called "*blouses*". They had been made of holland, checked or striped cotton and alpaca or wool in winter, loose with a belt or a sash which hooked behind, but carried out in different materials they became the new style of dress for young girls:

> "Blouses take the place of expensive dresses, though the latter for daily wear may be of the form of the blouse, the difference being in material and trimming."
>
> (*Ladies' Treasury*, 1880.)

The *Ladies' Treasury* in the same year spoke of "the lawn tennis

Nursery blouse, striped cotton. (*Ladies' Treasury*, 1880.)

pinafore" style which in London and its environs "has been adopted for children till it has culminated in a livery". Lawn tennis also brought another style into children's dress. In the late 1870s the decorative gauging which had for two or three generations ornamented the smock frocks of the English rural workers, entered fashionable dress, apparently first of all in dresses worn for lawn tennis and then in children's dress:

> "smocking so popular one or two years ago for lawn tennis costume has now found its way into children's dress".
>
> (*Queen*, 1880.)

The form of the smock frock and the blouse were like enough for the ornament of the former to seem the natural trimming for this new style for children. Weldons, the great instructors of the home dressmaker, issued several series of a booklet, *Practical Smocking*, which included miniature replicas of the country smock, with its non-functional embroidery as well as the decorative gathering. This was a passing fashion.

Yoked dress, with smocking, for girls of 2–10.
(*Weldon's Practical Smocking*, 1884.)

"The fancy of the moment is for children to wear the new provincial smock made exactly like the carters' or waggoners' dowlas frocks. . . . They are decidedly not becoming to little folks."

(*Ladies' Treasury*, 1880.)

A number of these small *smocks* can be seen today in museums. But the decorative gathering forming a yoke and controlling the fullness of the frock became a characteristic fashion of children's dress:

"How pretty are these old English smock frocks that have of late years become so fashionable for children of all ages."

(*Woman's World*, 1888.)

Not only everyday dresses of linen or cotton were treated in this way but also dresses of silk and fine wool for party wear.

"During the last few years little frocks of soft material, gathered or smocked on the shoulders, fastened below the waist with a soft silk sash have grown very much in favour with mothers who like to see their children comfortably and prettily dressed."

(Ibid., 1890.)

Smocking remained a popular ornament to the end of the century and for the dress of very young children has remained in fashion to the present day.

Dress falling loose from yoke, full sleeves with epaulettes. (*Housewife*, 1894.)

The reformers who had spoken strongly against the pressure of clothing at the waist and the general need for greater freedom welcomed the new styles. At first the "blouse" kept a loose waistline, which in the 1880s was low, and sometimes a pleated frill, forming a skirt, linked it with the fashionable style of dress. But by the late 1880s the dress fell loose and free from a yoke to the hem, the style which makes a complete divergence from adult fashion. Complaints about short sleeves now disappeared for the arms were now much more covered and comfortable, full sleeves also developed. Low-necked dresses disappeared, even for evening:

> "children rarely, if ever, appear now in low dresses, which is well, for they catch cold easily".

(Ibid., 1889.)

Bridesmaid's or party dress in voile and lace with silk sash. (*Housewife,* 1894.)

Accordion-pleated skirts appeared for party wear on the new yoked dresses from the late 1880s. The "blouse" or yoked form of dress was worn mainly by girls up to the age of 10, "For little girls from about four to nine the most universally approved styles are those having a yoke—either square or round—into which the material is gathered. No trimming is used at the hem, but three small tucks are useful for letting down at some future date and relieve the plainness" (*Enquire Within*, 1892). Above that age the waist was marked with a belt, and many of the dresses for younger children, although loose, keep the waistband, which was still in the early 1890s below the normal level. Fashionable details still appear. A schoolroom frock for a girl of 6 to 8 years old, described in *The Queen*, 1890, was yoked, but "with sleeves high on the shoulder, imparting to the frock a smart effect". A few years later the leg-of-mutton sleeve appeared in dresses for all ages. Another fashionable detail, the high, close-fitting collar, must have brought a new discomfort.

Coats also had the yoke and in the mid-1890s the full sleeves sometimes with epaulettes. Coats with capes were worn from the late 1880s. The hat of the 1890s could be either a variant of the sailor

Coat with cape, fur-trimmed, for a girl of 7–10. (*The Lady*, 1885.)

style, or a cross between this and the tam-o'-shanter in having a soft crown. There were wide-brimmed, flat-crowned hats, with both brim and crown soft and floppy, or the brims were stiffened with wire:

> "Hats for small children are of the picture class, being broad and bent into artistic forms, the crowns invariably of silk and satin and loose after the tam-o-shanter class. Much baby ribbon is used by way of garniture."
>
> (*Housewife*, 1895.)

These soft, flat-crowned hats were often of muslin or cotton for everyday wear. The elastic which held them under the chin was another remembered discomfort of these years. *Bonnets* were also worn.

The excitement of a new silk dress could not take away all the discomforts of a girl's clothing in the 1890s. The dress might be more comfortable to wear now, but there was still uncomfortable under-wear beneath:

> "The thought of the dress that awaited me in Peter Robinsons . . . the dress was a salmon pink surah with cream silk trimmings. . . . It was some comfort to slip the pretty dress on over the stiff, scratchy petticoats that were one of the minor tortures of my life. So was the hat elastic which left a red mark under my chin and when slipped behind my ears for relief made my head ache. So were the tight little kid gloves, worked down my fingers, till I could get my thumb in. So were the bronze boots now being buttoned over two pairs

Bonnet with frilled and lace trimmed brim, crown and curtain. (*Housewife,* 1895.)

of stockings, cashmere underneath and silk on top, so that I shouldn't take cold; because of this my insteps were pinched and my feet icy. But the new dress did look nice. . . ."

(Nursery in the Nineties, E. Farjeon, 1935.)

.   .   .

Girls at school were generally made to wear dresses sufficiently alike to give a uniform appearance, advertising the school, when they went for walks, paid visits or went to church. But the uniform of the fashionable academies did not, at the beginning of the century, have the intention of discouraging an interest in dress. There were also the charity schools, in which an older style of dress tended to be preserved, following still the instructions of the founder; or having individual garments changed at long intervals, so that at any time the dress might preserve part of a century-old style combined with more or less fashionable details. Miss Mitford describes this type of dress in *Our Village* when the village girl, at the age of 10:

"gets admission to a charity school, trips mincingly thither every morning dressed in the old-fashioned blue gown and white cap and tippet and bib and apron of that primitive institution, looking as demure as a Nun and as tidy. Then at twelve the little lass comes home again, uncapped, untippeted, unschooled."

The children of the dame school at Eckington in the 1830s were given a uniform dress of "poke bonnets dark prints and white tippets". Any divergence from it was frowned upon:

"I remember the intense disapproval of my mother and the teachers, at the dress of one girl who appeared in a bonnet adorned with artificial flowers, then considered quite unsuitable for school girls or servants."

(Two Generations, O. Sitwell, 1940.)

In *Jane Eyre*, Charlotte Brontë described the dress at Lowood:

"All with plain locks combed from their faces, not a curl visible; in brown dresses, made high and surrounded by a narrow tucker about the throat, with little pockets of holland (shaped something like a

Highlander's purse), tied in front of their frocks, and destined to serve the purpose of a work-bag; all wearing woollen stockings and country-made shoes, fastened with brass buckles."

Out of doors the girls wore:

"a coarse straw bonnet, with strings of coloured calico and a cloak of grey frieze".

Charlotte Brontë was no doubt remembering the dress she wore at the school at Casterton, which she left at the age of 9 in 1825. Mrs. Gaskell, in her *Life of Charlotte Brontë*, quotes the 1842 report of the school, which gave instructions for dress:

"The pupils all appear in the same dress. They wear plain straw cottage bonnets; in summer white frocks on Sundays, and nankeen on other days; in winter purple stuff frocks, and purple cloth cloaks. For the sake of uniformity, therefore, they are required to bring £3 in lieu of frocks, pelise, bonnet, tippet and frills."

Supervision sometimes extended to the person, as well as the garments. No doubt it was often with the best of hygienic intentions that the authorities decreed short hair in some of the schools, but most of our sympathies now would be with the shorn rebels of Ampthill:

"There has been a rebellion against hair-cutting which went so far that we were obliged to dismiss the ringleader who was a tall girl with a hideous thick yellow wig of which she seemed particularly fond. Now that she is gone the rest are rather awestruck, and gave up their heads to the executioner without even a sigh."

1840. (Cecilia Redway 1819-45.)

Lowood witnessed a similar scene, and hygiene was certainly not its inspiration there:

" 'What—*what* is that girl with curled hair? Red hair, ma'am, curled —curled all over? . . . And why has she, or any other, curled hair? Why, in defiance of every precept and principle of this house, does she conform to the world so openly . . . as to wear her hair one mass of curls?'

'Julia's hair curls naturally,' returned Miss Temple. . . .

PLATE 31

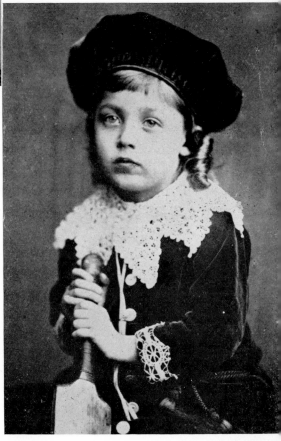

PLATE 32

Boy in jacket and knickerbockers, girls in highneck frocks with fringed borders—all wear elastic-sided boots. 1877.

From an original photograph

'Naturally. Yes, but we are not to conform to nature: I wish these girls to be children of Grace: and why that abundance? . . . Miss Temple that girl's hair must be cut off entirely; I will send a barber tomorrow.' "

And not only Julia, but all of them, who had their hair twisted into plaits and made into top-knots, plain though this was, were sentenced to have their hair cut off for the discouragement of vanity.

There was nothing in these uniforms specially designed for school life, which indeed at this time scarcely needed the freer dress which later was to set school uniform apart from normal fashion. It was not until the last quarter of the century that uniforms were influenced by the games and gymnastics which played an important part in the new girls' schools of this time. The introduction of daily drill, gymnastics and games in the curriculum of the new schools—the Girls Public Day School Trust was founded in 1873—made some modification of fashionable dress a necessity:

"There is advantage in the daily morning exercise besides the absolute rest it gives from brain work, and this is, that every girl is thus compelled to wear a dress loose and light enough for free movement, since it would not be possible for the whole school to change dress for the purpose. On special calisthenic days the girls are encouraged to wear a regular gymnastic dress of dark blue flannel, serge or other woollen material, with a light blue sash for the sake of uniformity, over which a skirt can be buttoned on at the waist and removed as they enter the gymnasium."

(At the North London Collegiate School, *Sylvia's Journal*, 1893.)

The Kindergarten costume recommended by the Rational Dress Society in the 1880s was woollen combinations; woollen stays—to button not to lace; woollen stockings, kept up by suspenders fastened to the stays; a divided skirt either buttoned on to the stays or made into a princess bodice; and a smock frock overall. For girls a little older a blouse beneath a sleeveless dress or pinafore gave the necessary freedom and this became the form of many school uniforms. Like some of the earlier school dresses these too, in time, preserved obsolete styles, the tendency of all uniforms.

C.C.E.–P

BIBLIOGRAPHY

Manuscript Sources

British Museum: Arundel MSS. 1220. *The Treatise of Walter de Biblesworth*. Early fourteenth century

Bedfordshire County Record Office: DDP 64/14; DDGA L/30/9/81; P 196/2

Essex County Record Office: D/DP.A

Kent Archives Office: Guilford M.S.S.

Lancashire Record Office: WCW 1640

Devizes Museum. *Wyndham Family Papers*

Public Record Office: *Wardrobe Accounts of Henry VIII*. Warrants E101 423/11/2

National Museum of Antiquities of Scotland: *Lord High Treasurer's Accounts* (Transcript)

Printed Manuscripts and Books

Acland, E. *Goodbye for the Present,* 1935

Archaeologia. Vol. 11 "Wardrobe Account of Prince Henry", 1608. Vol. 20 "Trousseau of Princess Joan", 1347

Babees Book, 1868

Benenden Letters, 1901

Blundell's Diary and Letter Book, 1952

Bedfordshire Letters of Bunyan's Day, 1955

Brudenells of Deene, J. Wake, 1963

Burrell, *Diary* of Timothy, Sussex Arch. Coll. III

Bulwer, J. *The Artificial Changeling,* 1650

Byrne, M. St. Clare. *The Elizabethan Home,* 1935

Cely Papers, 1475–88, 1900

Chesterfield Lord. *The World,* 1753

Clifford. *Diary of the Lady Anne, 1616–19,* 1924

Clive, Caroline. *Diary and Family Papers, 1801–73,* 1949

Cowper MSS. Hist. MSS. Comm., 1888

Du Maurier, D. *The Young George Du Maurier,* 1951

Delany, Mrs. *Autobiography and Correspondence,* 1861–2

Farjeon, E. *A Nursery in the Nineties,* 1935

Fell, Sarah. *Household Account Book, 1673–8,* 1902

Gale, Walter. *Journal of,* Sussex Arch. Coll. IX

Glenbervie Journals, 1910

Grant, Elizabeth. *Memoirs of a Highland Lady, 1797–1827,* 1950

Grose, F. *Antiquarian Repository,* 1775

Haldane, L. K. *Friends and Kindred,* 1961

Ham, Elizabeth, by Herself, 1783–1820, 1945

Hamilton, Mary. *Letters and Diaries, 1756–1816,* 1925

Harley. *Letters of the Lady Brilliana, 1625–43,* 1854

Hertford, Marquis of, "Purse Accounts", *Antiquaries Journal, XXV*

Holme, R. *Academie of Armourie,* 1688

Holroyd. *Girlhood of Maria Josepha, 1776–96,* 1896

Howard. *Household Books of Lord William, 1612–40,* 1877

Hughes, M. V. *A London Child of the Seventies,* 1934

Hutchinson, Sara. *Letters, 1800–35,* 1954

Hutton. *Life of William Hutton by himself,* 1816

Jerningham Letters, 1780–1843, 1896

Kemble, F. A. *Records of a Girlhood,* 1878

Londonderry, Marchioness of. *Frances Anne,* 1958

Mackenzie, Compton. *My Life and Times, Octave One,* 1961

Middleton MSS. Hist. MSS. Comm., 1911

Neville. *Diary of Sylas, 1767–88,* 1950

Nollekens and his Times, J. T. Smith, 1828

Oglander, A. Aspinall. *Admiral's Wife (Mrs. Boscawen),* 1940

Oxinden and Peyton Letters, 1642–70, 1937

Papendiek, Mrs. *Court and Private Life in the Time of Queen Charlotte,* 1886

Paston Letters, 1422–1509, 1872–5

Peacham, H. *The Truth of Our Times,* 1638

Penns and Penningtons of the Seventeenth Century, M. Webb, 1867

Porter. *Letters of Endymion, 1587–1649*

Ridley, Cecilia. *Life and Letters, 1819–45,* 1958

Roche, Sophie von la. *Sophie in London, 1783,* 1933

Rowlands, S. *Doctor Merry-Man,* 1616

Rowsell, Mary, *The Life Story of Charlotte de la Trémoille Countess of Derby,* 1905.

Sellars, E. *Edinburgh's Child*, 1961

Sibbald, *Memoirs of Susan, 1783–1812*, 1926

Slingsby, *Diary of Sir Henry, 1638–48*, 1836

Sitwell, O. *Two Generations*, 1940

Smith, J. T. *Book for a Rainy Day*, 1845

Stanley. *Early Married Life of Maria Josepha, Lady Stanley*, 1899

Stubbes, P. *Anatomy of Abuses in England in 1583*, 1882

Stonor Letters and Papers, 1290–1483, 1919

Thynne, F. *Animadversions, 1599*. Chaucer Soc. 1876

Tufnell, Samuel. *F. Steer*, 1960

Towle, M. *The Young Gentleman's and Lady's Private Tutor*, 1770

Verney letters of the Eighteenth Century, 1930: *Memoirs of the Verney Family during the Seventeenth Century*, 1892–9

Warner. W. *Albion's England*, 1606

Wycherley, W. *The Gentleman Dancing Master*, 1675

Williamson Letters, 174—65, 1954

Dress and Domestic Economy

Ballin, A. *The Science of Dress*, 1885

Dictionary of Daily Wants, 1861

Instructions for Cutting Out Apparel for the Poor, 1789

Lady's Economical Assistant, 1808

Merrifield, Mrs. *Dress as a Fine Art*, 1854

The Workwoman's Guide, 1838

Walsh, J. H. *Manual of Domestic Economy*, 1856

Weldon's Practical Baby Clothing, c. 1885

Cassell's Household Guide, 1868–70

Journals

Juvenile Magazine, 1788

Tailor and Cutter

Englishwoman's Domestic Magazine

Enquire Within

The Housewife

The Ladies' Treasury

The Lady's Newspaper

The Lady's World

Myra's Journal
The Queen
Sylvia's Journal
Woman's World

Secondary Sources
Bayne-Powell, R. *The English Child in the Eighteenth Century*, 1939
Cunnington, C. W. and P. *Handbook of English Mediaeval Costume*, 1952
    Handbook of English Costume in the 16th Century, 1954
    Handbook of English Costume in the 17th Century, 1955
    Handbook of English Costume in the 18th Century, 1957
    Handbook of English Costume in the 19th Century, 1959
    Dictionary of English Costume
Gardiner, D. *English Girlhood at School*, 1929
Godfrey, E. *English Children in the Olden Times*, 1907
Jackson, M. *What they Wore, a history of Children's Dress*
Moore, D. L. *The Child in Fashion*, 1953

INDEX

N.B. The italic numerals refer to illustrations.